SCHOOL ESSAYS, PARAGRAPHS, LETTERS, COMPREHENSION, TELEGRAMS AND ADVERTISEMENTS

[FOR SECONDARY CLASSES]

By

MADAN SOOD M.A.

(Formerly of Indian Air Force)

GOODWILL PUBLISHING HOUSE

B-3, RATTAN JYOTI, 18, RAJENDRA PLACE
NEW DELHI-110008 (INDIA)

Published by

Rajneesh Chowdhry
for
Goodwill Publishing House
B-3, Rattan Jyoti
18, Rajendra Place
New Delhi-110008
Tel : 25750801, 25755519, 25820556
Fax : 91-11-25763428
E-mail : goodwillpub@vsnl.net
Website : goodwillpublishinghouse.com

Typeset at

Radha Laserkraft
R-814, New Rajinder Nagar
New Delhi-110060 • Tel : 28742031

Printed at : Kumar Offset Printers, Delhi-110092

PREFACE

This book provides samples of different *genres* like Essays, Paragraphs, Letters, Comprehension, Telegrams and Advertisements and encompasses a wide range of composition writing and comprehension skills. It provides a wide source of themes ranging from a delineation of age-old problems to a discussion of contemporary issues.

There are variegated themes to motivate the learner to use English for purposes of communication and expression. A conscious effort has been made to provide interesting reading material — themes have been selected which would provide interest to students of ICSE, CBSE and general students as it aims at facilitating extra reading, for students of all standards are expected to read beyond the prescribed text books.

All categories of essays — Reflective, Narrative, Descriptive, Expository and Imaginative — find a place in this book. The Introduction Section provides a comprehensive background to the learners about the topics that have been dealt in the book.

As the comprehension of the given passage/s and subsequently to provide answers to the questions asked pertaining to the passage/s form part of more or less all the tests/examinations from Primary to Senior Secondary level and also of University and competitive examinations, since the real assessment of any examinee's calibre can be made only on evaluating the answers to the unseen passages where there is no scope for reproducing the already crammed answers, as may happen in the case of literature and to a certain extent in composition writing, exercises on comprehension will enable the students to fully gear themselves to solve any unseen passages which they may come across in their school tests or Board examinations. Exercises include very useful exercises on Practical Grammar/ Usage and answers to fully solved exercises have been provided to enable the students to evaluate their grasp of the topics.

This book will prove to be a boon for the young learners who are either taking up their academic examination or competing for a top job through competitive examinations. Keeping the needs of the students community in view and feeling the dearth of available books on the subjects, the present book amply serves the purpose.

MADAN SOOD

CONTENTS

CHAPTER 1

INTRODUCTION

PARAGRAPH WRITING

Chapters, Essays and other prose compositions are broken up into paragraphs to make their reading easier. The beginning of a new paragraph marks a change of topic, a step in the development of an argument or of a story. An essay would look uninteresting if it is not properly divided into paragraphs.

Definition

A number of sentences grouped together and relating to one topic, or a group of related sentences that develop a single point is called a paragraph.

Paragraphs may be short or long according to the necessity of the case. A paragraph may consist of a single sentence or many sentences.

Essentials of Paragraph Structure

1. Unity. Just as each sentence deals with one thought, each paragraph must deal with only one topic or idea. For example, in writing an essay, every head and every sub head, should have its own paragraph to itself. Every sentence in the paragraph must be closely connected with the main topic of the paragraph. The paragraph and every part of it must express one theme or topic. The topic, theme or subject of a paragraph is very often expressed in the first sentence of the paragraph and this sentence is called the key-sentence as it unlocks the subject to be dealt with in the paragraph.

2. Order. Order means logical sequence of thought or development of the subject. Events must be related in the order of their occurrence, and all ideas should be connected with the leading idea and arranged according to their importance or order.

The first and the last sentences are the two most important sentences in the paragraph. The first — the topical sentence — should arouse the interest of the reader and the last should satisfy it.

3. Variety. In order to avoid monotony, the paragraphs of a composition should be of different length and not always of the same sentence construction.

Single Paragraphs

The treatment so far has been of paragraphs which are parts of a lengthy composition like an essay or the chapter of a book. However, the students may be required to write short, separate paragraphs on subjects of ordinary interest. Such paragraph can be called miniature essays. The same principles as discussed above excepting the principle of variety, must be followed in their construction.

LETTER WRITING

The art of letter writing is not only an ornamental accomplishment but something that every educated person must acquire for practical reasons. Every literate person should know how to write a clear and readable letter.

There are several different kinds of letters such as friendly letters, business letters etc. and each of them has its own particular form. However, there are certain formats which apply to all and are explained below :

1. Heading consisting of (a) the writer's address and (b) the date.
2. Salutation

3. The body of the letter
4. The courteous leave-taking or conclusion
5. The signature
6. The superscription on the envelope

1. **The Heading.** The heading informs the reader where and when the letter was written. The *where* is the writer's full postal address and the *when* gives the date on which the letter was written.

Example

291 Sector V
Pushp Vihar
New Delhi-110017

15th November 2005

Note. The date may be written in full 15th November 2005 or abbreviated — Nov. 15, 2005 or 15-11-2005.

2. **Salutation.** Salutation or Greeting will depend upon the relation one stands to the person to whom one is writing. For example, to member of one's family, it will be — My dear Mother, Dear Mother, Dear Father, My dear Father, Dear Uncle etc.

To friends — Dear Des Raj, Dear Sohan etc.

To business people — Dear Sir, Gentlemen, etc.

Note. The use of the word 'dear' does not imply any special affection but it is a purely formal and polite expression.

3. **Body of the Letter.** The body of the letter will depend upon the kind of the letter one wishes to write and the style of the letter will differ considerably depending on to whom one is writing the letter. However, somc hints that apply to all letters are as under :

1. Letter should be divided into paragraphs unless it is very short, to mark changes of subject matter.

2. The language of the letter should be simple and direct, and the sentences should be short. Eloquence and long words should be avoided. One should be clear about what one wants to say and it should be said as directly as possible.
3. Think out what you want to say and before you start writing the letter, put down your points in some logical order.
4. Bad penmanship and slovenly writing should be avoided.
5. As the use of incorrect punctuation may alter the whole meaning of a sentence, commas, semicolons and fullstops should be put in their proper places.

4. **Conclusion.** A letter must not end abruptly simply with the writer's name. As this would look rude, certain forms of polite leave taking are prescribed, such as,

Your sincere friend,

Yours sincerely,

Yours truly, etc.

The subscription, or leave-taking phrase must be written below the last words of the letter and to the left side of the page.

Note. The first word of the subscription must begin with a capital letter; *e.g.*

Sincerely yours

5. **Signature.** The name of the writer or the signature must come below the subscription;

Yours very truly,

L.K. Handa

The signature should be clearly written in letters to strangers so that the reader may know whom to address in reply.

6. **Subscription.** The Superscription on the envelope may be as follows:

Shri K.L. Handa
38, Royal Street, Mumbai

Classification of Letters

Letters may be classified according to their different uses. They are :

1. Social Letters including Friendly letters and Notes of Invitations.
2. Business Letters including Letters of Application, Official Letters and Letters to Newspapers.

Social Letters

Just as in friendly talk, so in friendly letters one can touch on many subjects and in any order one likes. We can also use colloquial expressions which would be quite out of place in formal letters. Such letters written to relations and intimate friends should be written in an easy and conversational style and are, in fact, of the nature of friendly talk.

However, even such letters should not be badly composed and care should be taken to preserve some order in expressing our thoughts. Rules of spelling, punctuation, grammar and idiom should be adhered to while writing such letters.

Forms of Address

'Dear Father' or 'Mother', 'Dear Brother', 'Dearest Sister', 'Dear Ashok', 'My dear Sonu' etc.

It is respectful to use the title 'Shri', if you are writing to an ordinary friend who is much older than you *i.e.* 'My Dear Shri Tilak Raj Kapoor'.

Forms of Subscription

1. **Letters to Relatives and near friends.**

'Yours affectionately',
'Your affectionate/loving son',

'Your affectionate/loving brother',
'Your affectionate/loving friend'.

2. **To Friends.** Yours very sincerely.

Note. (i) While concluding letters to friends or acquaintances, whom you address as 'Shri', 'sincerely' or 'very sincerely' should be used in the subscription and this may be preceded by 'with kind regards'.

(ii) In letters beginning with the formal 'Dear Sir', sincerely should not be used and the proper word of subscription is 'faithfully or 'truly'.

Notes of Invitations

A formal invitation should contain no heading, no salutation and no complimentary close and is generally written in the third person. The writer's name should appear in the body of the letter. The address of the writer and the date should be written to the left, below the communication. The reply to such a note should repeat the date and time mentioned in the invitation and should also be in the third person. Informal notes of invitation, acceptance and refusal are like ordinary friendly letters, though using more formal language. They are addressed by name — 'My dear Shri Mongia' — and the formal close is usually any of the following:

'Yours sincerely',
'Sincerely yours',
'Yours affectionately',
'Yours very sincerely'.

Business Letters

As businessmen are busy men and have no time to read long and rambling letters, business letters should be terse, clear and to the point. Such letters are more formal in style than friendly letters.

The use of abbreviations should be avoided in business letters and care should be taken to ensure that 'subjects' are not omitted — "Have received" instead of "We have received".

While ordering goods in business letters, clear and exact descriptions of the articles wanted should be given and everything should be clear and precise.

The *form* of the business letters is the same as already discussed, with one addition, viz., the Address — the name of the firm or businessman to whom the letter is addressed.

Modes of Address vary According to Requirement

1. **To a tradesman**

    Sh. M.L. Sharma
    Bookseller
    12 Bank Street, New Delhi

Begin 'Dear Sir' and conclude 'Yours faithfully' or 'Yours truly'.

2. **To a firm**

    Messrs APS, M.S. & Co.
    56, Nariman Point
    Bombay

Begin 'Dear Sirs' or 'Gentlemen' and conclude with 'Yours faithfully'.

Note. If the firm has an impersonal title, 'Messrs' should not be prefixed. For example ABC Electronics, The Precision Pipes.

3. **To professional men** or **private gentlemen**

    Dr. Anand
    14, Qutab Road
    New Delhi

    Sh. R.K. Poply
    Solicitor
    Civil Lines
    Delhi

Begin 'Dear Sir' or 'My dear Sir', and conclude 'Yours faithfully', 'Yours truly' etc. (not 'Yours sincerely').

Note. When a business letter is signed by a clerk on behalf of his employer, he puts the letter p.p. (Latin *per pro* = on behalf of) before the signature of the firm, and writes has own initials beneath. For Example :

Yours faithfully
p.p. L. Charles & Sons
(M.S.)

Replies. In replying to a business letter, the number of reference (if there is one) and the date of the letter you are answering are always quoted. For example "This has reference to your letter No. 3824/PAT, dated December 25, 20..., I beg to say" etc.

Letters of Application

A letter applying for employment should have the following :

(i) A short introduction stating whether the writer is writing in response to an advertisement or is applying on his own responsibility.

(ii) A statement of age, educational qualification, experience, address, etc.

(iii) A conclusion giving references, testimonials and applicant's earnestness of purpose.

(iv) The form of letters of application should be the same as that of business letters.

Official Letters

In letters to officials, the proper form of address and subscription must be strictly attended to as such letters are the most formal of all and generally begin with — "I have the honour to call your attention to"; "I respectfully beg to report", etc. Name, titles and designation of the official to whom you are writing must be written in such letters. For example :

To

Sh. Ghan Shyam B.A. L.L.B., I.A.S.
Collector
Palampur

The letter must begin with the very formal "Sir" (not "Dear Sir", or "My dear Sir"). The proper subscription is :

Yours most faithfully
Rakesh Chauhan

Letters to Newspapers

These letters should always be addressed to 'The Editor', and should usually end with 'Yours truly'.

'Sir', and not 'Dear Sir', should be the proper form of salutation.

If his address is given by the writer for publication, it is usually placed below the letter to the left.

If the writer does not wish his name to be published, he can sign his letter with a nom de plume (such as "Interested", "Anxious", etc. but in any case his name and address must be given (in a covering letter) to the Editor, because anonymous letters will not be published by any respectable newspaper.

Comprehension

A comprehension exercise consists of a passage upon which questions are set so that the examinee's calibre and ability to understand the contents of the given text is tested, as to whether he understands the meanings and information given in the passage.

A few hints are given below :

1. In order to get the general idea, the passage should be read fairly quickly.
2. This should be followed by a second reading, a little slowly, so as to know the details.

3. Now study the questions thoroughly and then turn to the relevant portions of the passage. Read them again and then rewrite them in your own words.
4. Do not pick up the original language but write in your own style using your own words.
5. If meanings of any words or phrase are to be given, care should be taken to use the same part of speech as that of the asked word.

ESSAY WRITING

The word 'essay' literally means an *attempt* and an essay is an exercise in composition wherein you are to express your thoughts in good English. Precisely speaking, it is a written composition giving expression to one's own personal ideas or opinions on some topic. The term also covers any written composition, where it expresses personal opinions or gives information on any given subject, or details of a narrative or description.

Characteristics of a Good Essay

1. Unity. An essay must develop one theme with a definite purpose and the subject must be clearly defined in the mind and kept in view throughout. Anything which is irrelevant should not be admitted to the essay. However, the subject may be treated in a variety of ways and from different points of view.

2. Order. The essay should follow a certain order and come to a definite conclusion. Haphazard reflections should be avoided. It should have unity of subject and treatment.

3. Brevity. An essay, especially a school essay should not be long and it should be a brief exercise concisely expressed. However, the length of an essay will depend on the nature of the subject and there can be no strict rules regarding the length.

4. Style. The style of an essay must be more dignified and literary. Slang, colloquial terms and free and easy constructions should be avoided. The language and sentence construction of an essay should be simple, direct and natural.

5. Personal Touch. An essay should express the personal feelings and ideas of the writer, as an essay is a written composition giving expression to personal ideas or opinions on a subject. Without this personal touch, the essay will be colourless and devoid of individuality. Hence, it is better not to be afraid of expressing your own views instead of repeating the views of others.

Classification of Essays

1. **Reflective Essay.** A reflective essay consists of thoughts or reflections on some topic which is generally of an abstract nature.

For example : *qualities, habits etc.,* such as temperance, cowardice heroism; *domestic, political and social topics* such as family life, marriage, poverty, caste, riches etc., *philosophical subjects* such as reality, right and wrong and *religious and theological* topics.

While attempting such essays you should try to explain advantages of possessing good habits and disadvantages of not possessing them and references in support of your statements which should be supported with facts and arguments.

2. **Narrative essays.** In a narrative essay, an event or series of events are narrated. The subject for thought and comment is the narrative it relates. Narrative essays may treat *legends* or *historical stories, biographies, incidents* such as a street quarrel, an accident; *a journey* or *voyage; a story* which may be real or imaginary.

3. **Descriptive Essays.** They describe some *place* or *thing* —plants, animals, such as elephant, cow; *towns, buildings, countries* such a Paris, Delhi; *aspects and phenomena of nature* such as spring, monsoon, volcanoes; *manufactured articles* such as locomotives, paper, silk etc.

4. **Expository Essays.** An expository (which means explanatory) essay consists of an explanation or exposition of some subject—*occupations, industries, institutions* such as the Press, the Parliament etc.; *scientific topics* such as evolution, astronomy etc.; *literary topics* such as the novels of Charles Dickens, the genius of Shakespeare etc.

5. **Imaginative Essays.** Such topics as "If I were a millionaire", "The autobiography of a coin" come under Imaginative Essays. In such topics the writer has to place himself in imagination, in a position of which he has got no actual experience.

Hints on Essay Writing

Sometimes students feel that there is nothing to say about a subject and this is attributed to lack of experience and general reading. Therefore, if one wants to write good essays one must acquire *the habit of reading*. As all knowledge does not come from books, we should observe and learn much from life around us. We can also improve the skill of writing essays by *conversing with others*. Hence we should discuss subjects that interest us, with our friends and listen to people's conversation and should make them talk to us about the things they know.

You should have a *clear and accurate conception of the subject* of the essay before you attempt to write.

This should be followed by *collecting material* for your essay before you can write it. All essays should be *divided into paragraphs*. Essays not thus paragraphed look unattractive and are not easy to read.

Structure of an Essay — should have three parts — the *Introduction*, the *Body* of the Essay, and the *Conclusion*.

Make the Introduction of the essay *arresting*, keep the parts of the body of the essay in proper proportion and take pains in choosing words, constructing sentences and making paragraphs and make the conclusion effective and satisfying.

CHAPTER 2

ESSAYS

1. Secularism in India

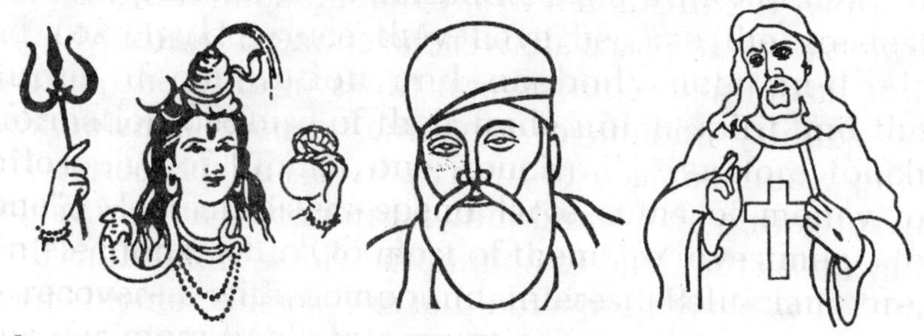

The Constitution of India specifically lays down that no citizen of the country shall be discriminated against on the basis of community, caste or creed. It clearly states that all people shall have the freedom to practise the religion of their choice without any interference from the State.

Inspite of the several divisive forces at work, India has been successful in maintaining its secular character. One would come across temples, mosques, gurudwaras and churches existing close to each other. People of different communities participate in each other's religious festivals and share the joy that comes out of fellow-feeling and innocent friendliness. They live together as equal citizens of a free India.

The reason for the country's adopting a secular set-up for the people basically lies in the fact that Indian culture stresses on respect not only for one's own religion but also respect and tolerance for other religions. No profession is barred to members of any community in India. Even the army and the police have members of the minority communities. Another reason why the framers of the Indian Constitution wanted to go in for secularism was that they wanted to make India a democratic State. The concept of democracy envisages freedom to the citizens in all their activities. Any other character for the Indian polity than the secular, would not have been suitable with the concept of democracy.

However, this is not to say that all communities have always lived in peace all over the country. Hindu-Muslim riots have broken out several times in different parts of the country and have sometimes caused considerable danger and damage to human lives and property. The investigating teams and judicial inquiries have revealed the causes that lead to communal riots. More often than not, it has been discovered that anti-social elements from the two communities were at the back of these riots. They first engineered a minor clash to begin with. Then they went on fraying the tempers of their respective communities. Thus, they succeeded in exciting them to acts of violence and revenge. Many a time, a misunderstanding over a small matter has also led to communal tension.

However, the most chronic cause of communal riots is the manoeuvring by politicians to gain political advantage out of the hostility between the two communities. Each political party wants to create and maintain vote banks for the purpose of winning elections. To this end they incite communal feelings. They keep reminding the people of their communal identity so that they can exploit these feelings at the time of elections. It is a pity that the secular nature of the Indian fabric is sought to be damaged by the vested interests for their narrow personal ends. The communal tension between the Hindus and the Sikhs in India is also political in nature. Left to themselves, the Sikhs and the Hindus have always lived in peace.

However, the redeeming feature is that these riots last only for a short time. Life does return to normalcy and the two communities begin to live in peace. This becomes possible because basically, there is no ill-will between the Hindus and Muslims or the Sikhs and the Hindus. Secularism can be further strengthened by the leaders of the two communities taking upon themselves the task to instil feelings of brotherhood and friendliness among their respective communities. ●

2. Race Prejudice or Apartheid

The belief that humanity has, by nature, been divided into races and subraces and that certain races are naturally superior to others in psychological endowment, forms the basis of the colour prejudice assumption. History reveals that the belief of racial superiority is very old and universal. In recent years outworn and forgotten racial theories have been revised in an attempt to rationalise political, social and economic actions and policies.

The white races consider that they are the true builders of civilisation. This concept shamelessly proclaims that white civilisation requires the legal barriers in order to protect itself against Asiatics and

Africans. It is true that white man should learn to treat every human being as their equal. There is no mystery about whiteness of the skin. It has been proved that given equal opportunity, a man, be of any colour or country is equal to any other. The white men should not forget that the greatest of the teachers of mankind were all Asiatics and they had no white skin. But it is regrettable that the whites in Rhodesia and South Africa behaved like brutes and enacted laws to force the Negroes, Indians and other Asiatics to live in horrid ghettoes. This is true of the USA that proclaims to be the most civilised nation in the world where the Bill of Civil Rights was treated as a scrap of paper in the Southern regions.

Non-violence is the dream of the wise, while violence is the history of man. In the twentieth century, violence was carried out by the groups of human species which took pride in being white, as if mere colour was the hallmark of superiority of race. It is a great stigma in human society because the discrimination between man and man can have no justifiable grounds. The study of the world history tells us the various causes of the colour prejudice. Various European powers established their colonies in Africa. The consequence of this policy of colonialism is the evil birth of racial discrimination.

Race prejudice, of course, has always existed in one form or the other. It has become more dangerous in the present times as there are weapons of mass destruction at the disposal of the rulers of the different countries of the world. Races which are scientifically advanced think that they have a right to dominate, govern and exploit people of the under-developed countries. Race prejudice shows that the animal in man still persists. The animals recognise the members of their own herd by scent but they react with suspicion at the approach of a strange animal even if it were one of their own species.

Human beings still possess many traits of animal behaviour.

Race prejudice will cause unparalleled human suffering as it has caused in the past. It was due to race prejudice that mass destruction of the Jews took place at the hands of the Nazis under Hitler. The Germans thought that they were a superior race and therefore must dominate the world. Hence the killing of millions of Jews.

A large section of the population called Negroes are treated as sub-human beings. Their children are refused admission in the so-called white schools, colleges, public places, restaurants and parks. When the Negroes seek their human rights, they receive bullets from the so-called superior race policemen. It was in America, the most developed and so called highly civilised country that the great leader Martin Luther King was killed.

In India, which has been the motherland of the exponents of racial harmony such as Lord Buddha, Sant Ravidas and Gandhiji, the racial prejudices are rampant. Gandhiji, who fought all his life for the uplift of the depressed classes and scheduled caste people, was assassinated by a communal fanatic. Incalculable harm has been done to humanity by the evil of race prejudice in different parts of the world. The cause of world peace has been greatly impaired due to the prevalent hatred between man and man. It has caused a severe blow to the progress of society and of the nations at large. It is heartening to note that by large, all over the world, people are raising their voice in protest against race prejudice. All the member countries of the UNO condemned the racial policies of the South African Government when it was ruled by the white regime. The enlightened section of the people in the USA has strongly condemned the racial prejudices of some of the states in their own country. ●

3. The Brain Drain Problem

The brain drain is a problem not peculiar to India, or even to the developing countries. Even much advanced countries have been losing some of their scientists to the U.S.A. But they lose only a few scientists who may have very personal reasons to go to the U.S.A. For India, brain-drain is a tremendous problem, far bigger than that of Britain or any other country. Various countries have adopted various methods to tackle it. Some countries give their scientists elite privileges and facilities and they just refuse to let them leave the country.

The Indian problem is much vaster and a selection board is no solution to it. There are various reasons which make these scientists quit. Money is certainly one factor. A young scientist who came back after a six-year distinguished record of research in the U.S.A., complained that as a pool officer in CSIR Scientists Pool, he got less than what he sent to his parents from the U.S.A. as a research worker. Unlike in the U.S.A. creation of special posts for distinguished scientists is a rare occurrence in India. It may take months and years of wrangling in committees.

Besides, there is the question of facilities, laboratories and equipment — all connected with money and foreign exchange. One may argue that the scarcity of resources makes us lag behind affluent countries like the U.S.A. However, this is not a sound reasoning. The fact remains that we give much less importance to education and research than the U.S.A. or other science-minded countries. Indian Universities have become cockpits of conflict and confrontation. It is unfortunate that the academicians should waste their energies in group rivalries and campus politics.

In such an atmosphere, it is no wonder that young people leave the country with hopes of better facilities and encouraging avenues abroad. Many of these young men have done remarkable work in the countries of their choice. There are many instances where scientists living abroad were lured back to India only to find themselves entangled in the bureaucratic cobwebs. They went back in a huff never to come back. The U.S.A. is the principal recipient of the rich 'drain' — a sizable number of them coming from the developing countries. UNESCO surveys reveal that among Indian specialists working abroad, 30 per cent are scientists and 54 per cent engineers. In New York alone, there are more U.S. trained Indian doctors than in the whole Iran.

The Government has been taking steps to see that some of the talented persons living abroad should come back to their hometown. Before expecting results, the Government should clean up the science administration. A sense of purpose and creativity should be injected into

Indian science. Non-residents of Indian origin who wish to set up industries in India have been offered facilities to import machinery and raw materials up to specified limits. This is aimed at attracting engineers and technicians settled abroad.

The outflow of a considerable section of young intellectuals certainly results in the poverty of the intellectual life of the nation. The community of politicians should keep off the field of science and leave it to the exclusive management by scientists. ●

4. Prohibition

Prohibition has been a controversial issue not only in India but the world over. Though drinking dates back to ancient times, this habit has been widely condemned in modern society. In the Bible, over 175 warnings have been recorded against drinking. Gandhiji firmly believed that liquor was "an invention of the Devil".

The Americans, who believe in enjoying life, enforced total prohibition in 1920 but they had to deliberately revert to the policy of non-prohibition. In India, the debate on whether drinking should be banned, has been going on even before independence. Many evils of drinking have been highlighted — the liquor, once consumed, makes a person lose control over himself. Intoxication takes away his rationality and makes him indulge in other evils such as gambling and prostitution. The drunkard becomes reckless and spends his hard-earned money received at the end of the day's labour on liquor. He is not worried about his wife and children who may be starving. He is not mindful of his own health. The craze for liquor becomes very acute. When a poor man cannot afford even the country liquor, sold at the licenced shops, he goes to the vendors of illicit liquor. One often hears of the mass tragedies, when many people, having consumed this brew, either become blind or die.

Furthermore, drinking takes away the energy of man. The hangover makes him lazy. He is not able to perform his job well. He lingers over his work or commits mistakes because his mind is clouded from the after-effects of liquor. He thinks of liquor even in the day. Thus, he is not able to concentrate on his work. There are some persons who drink even during the day and turn into economic parasites on the society. Regular drinking leads to weak nerves which make a person irritable and impatient. No doubt, after having consumed a few pegs, a drinker may get into a cheerful mood. He may even find release from stresses and strains of existence. But once the intoxication releases him, he is likely to become still more depressed and is gripped by nervous strain. Such a person is unlikely to prove to be a good, law-abiding citizen, a tolerant father and an understanding husband.

A bout of drinking may temporarily help an individual to free himself from tension but it is a fact supported by systematic surveys, that numerous crimes are committed in the state of drunkenness. Even family life gets affected if the head of the family falls prey to the habit of drinking. A drunk husband loses all sense of decency and control. In many poor families drunken husbands resort to wife-beating. Children feel deprived and grow up to be frustrated and bitter individuals. Even in educated homes, many a time, the drinking habit of the husband becomes the curse of marital happiness and ends in divorce.

There is, however, a section of the society which makes fun of the idea of prohibition and stands for freedom of individuals to drink. They argue that drinking, practised in moderation, proves rather beneficial for mental and physical health. If drinking were that harmful, a vast majority, all over the world, would not be that of drinkers. Furthermore, the champions of drinking point to the enormous loss of revenue that would be incurred by the State governments, if prohibition is enforced. Also, the cost of enforcing prohibition is tremendous. The practical experience of prohibition, when it was enforced in Maharashtra by the then Chief Minister, resulted in illicit distillations, wide-spread corruption among the enforcement staff, gangsterism and terrorism. Therefore after some years, the prohibition policy had to be reversed. The same was the case in Haryana. It is also pointed out that if people are prevented from drinking, they might take to more dangerous forms of intoxication such as heroin, LSD, ganja and opium which will certainly do more harm to the human system than a couple of pints of liquor.

However, it is far from advisable to allow people to go on drinking freely and burning their money and injuring their health. It is certain that as and when prohibition is introduced, it will do tremendous good, both, to the people and to the nation at large. ●

5. The Value of Travelling

Curiosity is one of the characteristics of man which can never be satisfied. In all ages men have wanted to know about things and places. In order to acquire knowledge, they have studied books and travelled in the face of several hazards. It was the keen desire to wander and see places that led Columbus and Vasco da Gama to discover America and India. When printing had not developed, and newspapers were not available, travellers played a crucial role. People of a city or a village gathered news about the happenings in other parts of the country from these travellers. Also, these travellers related the details of the different styles of living of people in different places and the listeners learned what they could not gather from any other source.

Travel is both a source of education and an enjoyable experience. No amount of description of a place or people in books can be a substitute to a personal visit to the place concerned. The impact of seeing it for oneself is much more than merely reading about it. Generally, when we get into the routine of travelling from our residence to our place of work, we begin to lose interest in our surroundings. We seldom notice any changes that take place on the route. Travelling, on the other hand, sharpens our power of observation. When, we are at a new place, we tend to get interested in the unfamiliar details of the place. Our curiosity about the new place makes us alert and we start taking mental note of the surroundings.

Leading the life of a frog in the well narrows our mental horizons and we begin to regard our narrow limits as the whole world. Travelling brings us face to face with the variety that exists in this vast world. We meet people speaking different languages, eating different foods, wearing different dresses and observing life styles which have nothing in common with those of our own. We exchange ideas with other people. We find that there can be more than one way of dressing up and the other ways are not necessarily inferior to those of our own. We may, at times, learn and benefit from the study of political and social institutions prevailing in other countries.

Several problems arise from the fact that people of different regions in the country seldom find an opportunity to visit regions other than their own. They can learn and understand at first hand about the true nature of the problems of a particular region. When one looks at a problem from another's point of view, one understands and realises the unreasonableness of one's own stand.

Travel brings alive the historical and other monuments. We generally read about them in books, but they remain in our minds as only abstract word-masses. When we are face to face with the monuments about which we have read, we experience a thrill, which is not to be got through books at all. Travelling also satisfies the spirit of adventure in us. Visiting far-flung places, sometimes not easily connected by transport, entails difficulties. But therein lies the thrill of having conquered the distance. There is something in man which drives him towards tackling challenges and travelling fulfils this urge.

Besides being a source of instruction and education, travelling also provides joy and pleasure. The thrill of being at a new place, amidst strange people and sharing exotic food with them is something which cannot be adequately put into words. While travelling one finds oneself released from the constraints of time and space. The unique sense of freedom is indeed joyful.

Last but not the least, the illiterate who cannot learn from books, can also educate themselves by travelling and observing things. Actually, the knowledge acquired by an illiterate person by visiting different places would be much more meaningful to him. It will remain with him for the rest of his life, as against the bookish knowledge which may sometimes leave some doubts in the mind of the reader. More and more people, for all these reasons, are taking to travelling. ●

6. The Press — Its Functions and Responsibilities

The first newspaper in India on modern lines appeared in Kolkata on 27th January 1790. This was the *Bengal Gazette*, published in English by an Englishman, J.A. Hickey. Today there are more than 2000 dailies (all languages) more than 200 tri-weeklies, 1000 weeklies, 1500 monthlies and more than 1500 others.

The Press plays an important role, both in the affairs of the nation and the lives of the people. The power of the Press has been equalled to that of Parliament and the Judiciary. The Press can make or mar the fortunes of a political party or an individual politician. It can raise the

ordinary individual to a high position for his act of bravery, honesty and patriotism. Conversely, it can expose the misdeeds of a smuggler or corrupt politician. It can incite the public and put it on the warpath against the government. But it can also instil appreciation of the governmental achievements and projects. This is why, the Press, especially in a democratic set-up, has to follow certain norms and has to exercise objectivity and restraint in order to play a healthy and constructive role.

Newspapers form an important link with the outside world. They provide the common man information about important events like earthquake, air crash, dacoity, floods, results of an election, outbreak of epidemic. They also tell us about the weather, the sunrise, temperature on each day. They inform us about the various entertainment programmes like, films, drama, music concerts etc. There are several other kinds of advertisements which are of use to the readers. The 'Situations Vacant' columns help the job-seekers. The 'Matrimonial' columns help the anxious parents to find suitable matches for their sons and daughters. Sale and purchase of property is conducted through the newspapers. Thus, the newspapers occupy on important position in the lives of the people. We begin to feel uneasy if we do not get our newspaper on time and everyday.

One of the most important functions of newspapers is to report objectively all the national and international events. Reporting should be unbiased, for an untrue news item can do great harm by provoking the public. Similarly, unbalanced reporting of international events can cause unnecessary ill-feeling between the governments and the people of the two concerned countries. Since the newspapers are a powerful medium of propaganda, sometimes different political parties start and finance newspapers. Their motive is to protect their own ideology at the cost of objectivity.

Few people are able to form their own judgements about the national issues and policies adopted by the government. Fewer still are capable to interpreting and analysing the issues in order to see them in the right perspective. Newspapers perform these important tasks through editorials. They give opinions on different current affairs. Forming of public opinion is therefore an important function of the Press. Here, the newspaper must play an impartial role. There are cases of removal of editors from their posts when they tried to resist the management pressure, as the big business houses owning some of the national dailies, may have certain vested interests.

Newspapers also act as forums of public opinion. Each national daily and small newspaper devotes space to letters to the Editor. These letters highlight the problems being faced by people, the weaknesses of the law and order, lack of civic amenities and so on. Once a letter to the Editor is published, it attracts the attention of the relevant authorities. They try to remedy the wrong so that their name is not spoiled by adverse publicity.

Newspapers, in a democracy, perform a very important task of acting as a watchdog of people's interests. They act as champions of democratic traditions. Through the lead articles, the newspapers present commentaries on policies and practices of the government and inform, arouse and mould public opinion. Specialists in particular fields, academicians and political scientists present in-depth studies in these lead articles which are by and large balanced, informed and fair. Pressmen, however, sometimes err. At times, it is done consciously when selfish motives may be behind publishing a distorted news items. At other times, it may be done unconsciously when a story is filed by a reporter without verifying the facts. In such cases, the published reports constitute misinformation and can cause damage to the reputation of an individual or an institution. As it is inconceivable to curb the freedom of the Press, it should not report or publish any news item which runs counter to the freedom of the Press. ●

7. Urbanisation or The Slum Problem

There is a continuous flow of people into cities from the villages. This is particularly true of big cities. Cities like Mumbai, Kolkata, Chennai and Delhi are among the highest density cities. They have actually become hives overcrowding with human beings.

Large-scale urbanisation leads to several complications in cities. Civic amenities fall short of needs. Law and order problem becomes worse. Prices of essential commodities shoot up. Most important of all, the housing problem becomes acute. The house-rents go very high. Middle class people find it difficult to afford the high rents. The lower-income groups find it impossible to live in comfortable houses. The outcome of this is slums in cities. They become widespread and are to be found in almost all parts of cities. Many a time, these slums come up right under the shadows of posh palaces and multi-storeyed buildings.

Several factors are responsible for people rushing to cities. The first and foremost is the population explosion. Because of increased population, the area of arable land has become inadequate. It can no longer feed all the inhabitants in the villages. All villagers are not landowners. Earlier, a large majority used to survive as agricultural labour. As their number has increased, not all of them are needed as agricultural labour. So, they leave for the neighbouring cities in search of work. Most of them find work in the cities as unskilled labourers. Their women folk also join them. Many of them get work as construction workers or get jobs as house-maids. They somehow find means of survival. This section of population begins by sleeping on the pavements. Then gradually they build shelters for themselves in jhuggis. These jhuggis become regular shelters after some time.

Industrialisation and technological progress are also responsible for the increasing urbanisation. More and more large-scale and small-scale industries are set up in and around cities and their number always increases. They need a large labour force which comes from the neighbouring villages. An opportunity to get a regular job in a factory with a regular income is welcomed by landless workers. They find these jobs profitable and readily leave their homes. Over the years, they call their relatives and friends to get jobs in the factories. With the result the cities expand.

The village young folks are getting increased opportunities for education. Their attitude to agriculture as a source of livelihood has changed. These young men do not want to continue with the vocation of their forefathers. After acquiring a graduation degree, they regard agriculture as below their dignity. So, they also rush to cities to seek jobs as clerks. The city population goes up and the city has to expand. Slowly, the surrounding villages get absorbed in the cities and are urbanised. Among other factors, the lure of the city, the glamour of the multi-storeyed buildings and the hustle and bustle of the city also attract some villagers. They come to cities with the intention of sharing the thrills of city life. Having come to the city they get disillusioned. They have to live in unhygienic slums. They sometimes curse their stars for having left their village homes but by then it is too late and they can not return to their village. They become part of the large crowds in the cities. All these factors, over the years have led to increasing urbanisation. Slums have become regular features of the cities. These slums lack even the basic necessities of life — fresh drinking water, electricity, public amenities. There is slush all round because of open drains.

The Central Government has been conscious of the sad condition of the slum-dwellers. However, it will not be an easy task to abolish the slums from the face of cities altogether. The present slum-dwellers are given alternative accommodation. But more people keep on pouring into the cities. So long as poverty and unemployment in villages persist, the unemployed landless labourers will continue to run to cities. ●

8. Violence

Human civilisation has come a long way from the Stone Age, yet man continues to be violent, in his conduct. In the early stages of man's development, men could survive only by violence. They had to use violence against wild and fierce beasts amidst which they lived. Violence against each other was also practised. There was not much communication between groups of men and they were suspicious of each other's intentions. Therefore, they attacked each other frequently. Violence then was, a way of life, dictated by the force of circumstances. But unfortunately and strangely, even today violence is prevailing in the conduct of human affairs and humanity seems to be feeling shaky under the impact of violence.

Man has not learnt any lessons from the two World Wars which brought about untold sufferings and destruction of men and materials. The scars of World War II are still present. Hiroshima and Nagasaki still remind the world of the damage that was caused by violence. The Israel-Arab violence is still going on and has resulted in deaths of uncountable men, women and even children. There was massive violence in Palestine, Lebanon, Iran and Iraq. The killing of thousands of men, women and children in Iraq as a result of the U.S. attack is a strong reminder of the allround violence.

In South Africa, the white regime unleashed violence on the blacks,, in their own home. Vietnam, Kampuchea, Grenada, Afghanistan, Falklands, Bangladesh and Sri Lanka, all have witnessed massive violence and destruction.

Within India too, one can witness spread of violence. Communal riots in various parts of the country including the recent violence in Gujarat have claimed many lives, besides a heavy destruction of property. There has been massive violence in Punjab and in Jammu and Kashmir where the sea-saw battle between the para-military forces and terrorist outfits has never stopped from the day of its beginning. Apart from these, one witnesses violence in other spheres of life. Students indulge in violence for the most trivial demands and destroy property and beat up teachers. In-laws burn their daughters-in-law because they have not brought enough dowry. Anti-social elements indulge in violence with impunity.

But why is violence on the increase ? Increasing materialism has made man selfish. It has also made him insensitive to human emotions of pity, compassion, generosity and affection. Nations want to expand their territory and influence. Men want to prosper materially at whatever cost. A rat race for material success is afoot, in which humans are ruthlessly trampling under foot their fellow-runners. Cut-throat competition is being practised in order to amass wealth. Exploitation of the worst kind is being practised by man on man, simply to become richer.

Lust for power is another factor that has increased violence. The U.S.A. and other super powers are competing with one another to increase their fire-power and their areas of influence. Occasionally, they also resort to direct violent actions in some of the underdeveloped countries with a view to establishing a puppet government there. Hitler was a power maniac, but the present-day rulers are no less power hungry. They would do anything to increase their spheres of power. With the scientific and technological advancement, mankind has come to possess newer and more destructive weapons. Nuclear energy, being diverted to destructive channels, has increased the fire-powers of the countries manifold. It is a common psychological fact that the possession of weapons makes individuals and nations haughty and aggressive.

In the modern times, religion and spirituality are at a discount and hence nations of the world have become less tolerant. There is little humility and inflated egoism. It is through religion and spirituality that significance of non-violence is grasped. As all human beings are representations of God, we will love God's creations only if we respect God. If this philosophy and outlook is adopted in life, violence is automatically eliminated from the world. World peace then becomes a reality. Men can then lead secure and peaceful lives.

However, religion is regarded as the opium of the masses and a hindrance to scientific progress. It is a fact that today man is his own greatest enemy. By unleashing the animal in him, man is torturing himself with violence. If mankind is to survive, violence will have to be discarded and a spirit of friendly co-existence will have to be made the norm of human behaviour. ●

9. Adult Education

More than five decades have passed since India achieved independence from the British. Still India remains a backward country because more than fifty percent of India's population is illiterate. India is a vast country and achieving cent per cent literacy has not been possible.

After independence, there has been a considerable increase in the number of schools and colleges and the number of students who have acquired education in these institutions has also increased tremendously.

However, most of our people are still illiterate and they can not afford to send their children to school. There is extreme poverty and also lack of awareness about the importance of education. There is a slow increase in the rate of literacy.

The need to launch a programme, to educate the adults of our country, was therefore felt immediately after independence. The idea was mooted by the father of the nation, Mahatama Gandhi. A nation-wide National Adult Programme was launched on 2nd October 1978 on the birthday of Mahatma Gandhi, with the help of Union Education Department and the State Education Services. The programme aimed at making the illiterate masses of India aware of the value of education. Teachers were sent to the homes of the learners, incentives were given to the learners who were explained the importance of education. The help of highly dedicated persons was sought to implement the programme of adult literacy. Also, the help of radio, T.V. and various village development unions was taken on large scale to make the programme a success. People in large numbers came forward to render help to the learners and the learners also cooperated. The results were not satisfactory.

There are many reasons. Firstly, India is a very large country and the problem is acute. Most of the illiterate adults are not ready to devote time to education. They want to give this time to the earning of their livelihood. The government is not able to provide sufficient funds for the implementation of the programme of Adult Education. At some places, the scheme is only on paper and nothing is being done to launch it in practice. It is very difficult to convince the poorest of the poor that they should acquire some literacy or some fundamentals of education before they start earning their livelihood. Hence, the programme has not met with success.

There is, however no doubt that the Adult Education programme has borne some fruit. Many people in cities and villages have taken advantage of it. Many farmers, workers, women and artisans are now able to read newspapers and keep their personal accounts. Though the programme has not been able to gain much popularity among the masses of India, the results have not been very disappointing. India really needs Adult Education movement. It can certainly achieve massive success if the Government and non-government bodies come forward and extend their whole-hearted support. ●

10. An Ideal Student

Young men and young women are the wealth of a nation. Ideal students are rare gems among the youth. They can bring laurels to their country. In ideal student is one who considers study his first love. He is hard-working and is ever eager to acquire more and more knowledge. He is obedient and punctual and always fully attentive to the teacher in the class room. He is not merely satisfied with studying the prescribed text books. As he has thirst for knowledge, he reads books outside the syllabus.

An ideal student can very aptly be compared to a blotting paper. He tries to learn good things from every person and tries his level best to have an all-round personality. He believes in simple living and high thinking. He is studious but not a book-worm.

An ideal student is a source of delight to his parents. He is respectful to his teachers and parents and does not waste the hard-earned money of his parents. The teachers are proud of an ideal student who considers his teachers his true guides. He is fully conscious to the fact that his teachers have his welfare at heart. He is the hope of the nation and the leader of the nation in the years to come.

Through his qualities of head and heart, he becomes an object of envy and admiration. His conduct is worthy of emulation. An ideal student is a true gentleman who possesses good manners and never loses his temper. He remains cheerful under all circumstances. He does not hit any body below the belt. He is fair and square in his dealings with others. He is always eager to help others and he tries to do a good turn to others every day.

An ideal student is an asset to his parents, his educational institution, his state and his country. With his polished manners and speech, he wins the hearts of all who are around. He bears a good moral character. He is not a broken reed and is dependable for his sterling qualities of character. He is honest and sincere and shuns bad company. He has an optimistic outlook on life. He does not waste his time in idle gossip. An ideal student is a true patriot and at the call of the country, he is prepared to sacrifice his life. Gradually he grows into an ideal citizen and is an asset to the country.

No gold but only men can make
A people great and strong
Men who for truth and honour's sake
Stand fast and suffer long. ●

11. Should Death Penalty be Abolished ?

Whether an assassin be sentenced to death or he should be given a prison sentence for life ? Will the abolition of death penalty result in a sharp increase in the number of murders ? These and similar other questions keep agitating the minds of right-thinking persons all over the world after England took the initiative and abolished death penalty.

Since the beginning of the organised society, capital punishment has been there. In olden days, the prevalent idea was : an eye for an eye and a tooth for a tooth. If a man took the life of another man, society took the life of the murderer. Such blood-thirsty punishments are no more in tune with the present civilisation. Death punishment cannot be justified on moral or ethical grounds. Is not the judge who awards the death sentence, as great a murderer whom he is sending to the gallows ?

Different methods are used to finish the life of a criminal. The most prevalent are hanging by rope and administering of electric shocks. Some military offenders and condemned political prisoners have to face the firing squad to meet their death. In Italy, war-time dictator, Mussolini was killed by a firing squad. In the olden days, the criminals were beheaded. The head of King Charles I was cut off by a hangman's axe. Whatever the method is followed to put an end to the life of a criminal, it is revolting and reminds us of the days of barbarism.

More than thirty-five countries have abolished death penalty and the aftermath of it has done no harm to the society. After India got her independence from the British yoke, Ratan Bai Jain was the first woman to be hanged in India's capital. Most of the persons are of the view that punishment should either be reformative or deterrent but death sentence is neither. It cannot reform the criminal since he is dead and is beyond good and bad. Murder is committed by the murderer in the heat of the moment and he is completely reckless about the consequences of his action. Some people are of the view that spending one's whole life in prison is a more severe punishment than hanging.

About three centuries ago, there were some two hundred crimes for which the punishment was death. Today murder is the only crime that is punishable with death. The thieves were warned through public hanging in the olden days. But while one thief was being hanged, other thieves were busy pick-pocketing in the crowd collected there. Also, there is the element of human error. There have been cases were innocent men were sentenced to death and the real culprits were found later.

When hundred of crimes were punishable with death penalty, people thought that if death sentence was abolished, there would be no fear and hence the crimes would increase. Today, death sentence has been abolished for all crimes except murder yet there is no wholescale chaos and anarchy as feared by people. Also, there is widespread misuse of death penalty to kill one's political rivals. A bogus case is put up in the court, a sham trial is held and the judge sentences the person to death. At the end of World War II, Hitler committed suicide and his great companions were hanged by the order of the War Crimes Tribunal. Their chief crime was that they had been defeated in the war, though the victorious side had done the same acts.

The present era is not that of barbarism and therefore the barbarous punishment of death should be abolished. Murderers are not inborn murderers. In fact, they are so because of the circumstances in which they are placed. The society, education, employment opportunities and many other reasons are responsible in turning ordinary human beings into criminals. Even criminals possess something good as a trait in their personality. Hence death penalty is no way to reform criminals. ●

12. Generation Gap

Change is the law of nature. There has to be and will always be some kind of difference between two generations. The generation gap is a universal phenomenon and is not peculiar to our country alone. The old order changes yielding place to new lest one good custom should corrupt the world. Everything is subject to change. Man's attitude, his thinking habits, eating and drinking habits and even fashions in dress change. Nothing remains static in a society. Ezra Pound rightly remarked :

"Go to the adolescents who are smothered in family —
Oh how hideous it is
Those three generations of one house gathered together
It is like an old tree with shoots
And with some branches rotted and falling.

These days, the generation gap is getting wider, especially in richer countries where parents are unable to look after their children because of pre-occupations and several business activities. As a result, children are neglected. For want of proper parental care and affection, children go astray. An adolescent can not tolerate parental indifference. Adolescents become rebellious and bid good-bye to the established order. They seek refuge in sex, drugs and in violation of the established order.

In India, parents are, by and large, authoritative and foist their views and opinions on their children, in matters of education, choice of profession, choice of a marriage partner and so on. The children feel that their parents are tyrannical in these matters. Parents think that they are the best judges while choosing their sons-in-law or daughters-in-law. If children try to assert their own choice in the matter of a life partner or in the choice of a profession, they are branded as rebels.

The young people feel that their parents are unreasonable and orthodox. The son wants to be an engineer or an MBA but the father insists that the son should compete for the IAS and other competitive examinations. Parents, sometimes, do not care about the children's choice and idealism. The break-up of the joint family system is closely related with the question of generation gap. Young people find it difficult to stay with old fogies who have orthodox, hide-bound views. Generation gap can be bridged if the elderly people treat the young with sympathy and understanding. They should be willing to accommodate the view-point of the younger generation. The elder generation is supposed to be mature, far-sighted and experienced whereas the young people are ignorant, rash, impetuous and defiant. The elders should, therefore adopt a reasonable attitude. Instead of dubbing the youngster's attitude as rebellious and heretic, they should try to tackle them in a friendly way.

The relationship between the old and the young generations should be the host-guest relationship. If this relationship is observed, generation gap can be bridged to a great extent. ●

13. Our Cultural Heritage

India has rich cultural tradition and there is a smooth blending of art, religion and philosophy in the Indian culture. Indian culture is actually an outcome of continuous combination and has absorbed many external influences in the course of history. From the ancient times till recent past, we were exposed to an unbroken sequence of civilisations. The flexibility of Indian culture has enabled it to survive foreign invasions and retain its originality and traditional character.

Indian people are tolerant and fatalists by nature and have at no time ridiculed the traditions of foreign civilisations. In fact, the Indian mind has absorbed much of the thinking of the other cultures, thus enriching itself and thereby becoming unique in character. The wisdom of our ancient epics like 'Ramayana' and 'Mahabharta' serves as a beacon light to the seekers of spiritual joy. Lord Buddha taught us to follow 'the middle path' by exercising control over passions. Indian sages and philosophers had started thinking on great issues more than three centuries ago which were raised in the West only in the last century.

Indian art was influenced by the religious beliefs and the philosophical trends of the times. The temples of the south, the caves of Ajanta, Ellora and Khajuraho are living testimony to the artistic excellence achieved by the Indian artists, sculptors and architects in those bygone days. Foreign tourists experience a spiritual reawakening on visiting these places. Indian music is remarkable because of the continuity in its growth. Like Indian dance, it is built on the concepts of 'ragas' and 'talas'. Each raga is regarded as appropriate to certain emotion, a certain mood suitable for a certain time of the day or night.

The background of Indian dance is infinitely rich and varied, as varied as the land itself yet with the same underlying unity which binds the people of the country together. The dances of India, whether folk or classical are an eloquent expression of an ancient civilisation. The timeless wisdom of our ancient civilisation continues to evoke the passionate search of man for conscious identity with God.

Since independence, Indian themselves have become increasingly keen to promote their sense of national identity and cultural unity. As a result, there has been a revival of interest in native folk arts, especially in the realm of music and dance. Now, it is up to our educational institutions to ensure that the younger generations imbibe the right values and try to uphold the torch of spiritual and cultural revival for the rest of the world to see and follow, and not to get carried away by the materialistic ideology.

We must ensure that modern India does not at any stage forget its rich cultural heritage — a legacy of our ancient seers, philosophers and sages. The success with which programmes like 'Festivals of India' have met with in the U.S.A., France and other countries proves the interest of the foreigners in our cultural traditions. The classical theatre has a tradition of more than two thousand years. These were mainly performed on platforms raised in temple courtyards and palaces. With the passing of early Hindu kingdoms — under whose encouragement the arts had flourished in India — and the Muslim invasion of the North, the tradition of drama almost died in the North. However, southern India retained a remarkable continuity of its cultural heritage because of its geographical position where the foreign invaders did not meet with much success.

The British Raj to a certain extent was responsible for the recovery of intellectual curiosity. A deep interest was taken in the story of India's past and to preserve the country's rich cultural heritage. It was a sign of maturity and foresight on the part of the British to leave the people to follow their faiths and beliefs. All these are attempts to keep our cultural heritage alive and it on to the younger generations. ●

14. Unity in Diversity

India is a vast country comprising many racial groups. There is great number of spoken languages, dialects and regional variations. The people of India profess and practise different faiths according to their beliefs which reflect in their customs, rituals, morals, norms, dress, festivals etc. The unique feature that emerges from this diversity is that in spite of all this, they are essentially united. Though several foreign invaders have attacked India, yet none ever succeeded in destroying the basic Indian culture.

After independence, our Constitution declared India as a secular State. It has great reverence for all the faiths and gives all its citizens freedom to profess and practise their religious beliefs. It does not recognise any distinction based on religion, race, sex, caste or colour. In the early days of the struggle for independence, people from all walks of life, with diverse religious, cultural, social, economic and linguistic backgrounds, stood united in their determination to throw the British out of the country. Even in the immediate past, during two wars with Pakistan and one with China, the entire nation stood as one behind its armed forces to boost their morale.

Indian civilisation has always been based on religious and moral values. Herein lies its unity and strength. In all parts of the country, cultural unity and the unity of the way of life and outlook surpasses the vast diversity in faith, beliefs and practices. One may travel from one end of the country to another and encounter a totally different social environment, where people talk, dress, worship differently, yet one will not feel a stranger. Everywhere, he will recognise a common thread in some aspect of life which makes him feel at home. Indian culture has preserved its fundamental character through the ages.

In spite of this, we cannot keep our eyes closed to the reality. Certain anti-national and external forces are trying to disturb the unity of the country by inciting communal feelings and sentiments. These are disturbed times. There has been increasing intolerance, disharmony and lawlessness. There have been riots and killings of innocent people. These incidents have terrorised people. In panic, when people face threat to their lives, they tend to cling to their socio-religious groups which leads to distrust of the intentions of other people belonging to different communities. Violence should not be allowed to raise its ugly head and destroy our unity. When a country is torn by internal strife, there is always a danger of external aggression.

Today Indian culture is in a state of change and progress. The winds of change in the wake of rapid advancement of science and technology have swept over the entire world including India. However, there should not be an indiscriminate following of the western modes, to the utter disregard of what suits the nation. People should not be allowed to forget their own cultural and social heritage. Today, educated youth is exposed to western culture and has started adopting the western life-style—western fashion, tastes, dress, fast foods etc. — and have created a big gulf between themselves and the rural masses. This trend should be checked.

It is universally accepted that science and technology should be increasingly used to raise productivity, standard of living of the people, reform the existing social structure. It is also felt that only when we have combined these with our values, can we achieve success and guarantee a balance between tradition and modernity. Only then can we retain the distinction of being a country unique for maintaining unity in spite of diversity. Attempts should be made to strengthen the common bond of unity that ties the people together in spite of the diversity in their beliefs, ways and religion. ●

15. Terrorism

In any set-up there are legitimate, legal and peaceful means of expressing displeasure and disapproval of certain policies of the rulers. By non-violent means, a group of individuals can attract the attention of the government and put forward their demands. Peaceful demonstrations, dharnas, *satyagrah*, strikes and non-cooperation movements are some of the methods successfully employed by Gandhiji in India and Martin Luther King in the U.S.

However, of late, a different method has come into existence. This is terrorism. A group of individuals decide to press for their demands by terrorising people and the governments. They do so by indulging in violent activities in a secret way. They plant bombs and other explosive devices at public places, kill men, women and even children and destroy property. They blow up the railway tracks to blow up trains. They kill important political figures to strike terror among masses. They also indulge in mass killings. They hijack to press for their demands. Sometimes, they form suicide squads which go about killing people and wreaking destruction by tying up bombs to their bodies. Terrorism has become a wide-spread and world-wide phenomenon. There have been terrorist activities in Palestine, Britain, Sri Lanka, the U.S.A., Arab countries, Isreal, India, Pakistan and it seems that by and large, all parts of the world are affected by this menace of terrorism to a lesser or greater degree.

Tackling terrorism has become one of the most important tasks of several governments of the world. The terrorists should be firmly dealt with. The government needs to tone up the Intelligence Wing of the police so that information about their activities can be obtained and pre-emptive action taken. Besides, there should be strict, comprehensive and foolproof laws to bring the terrorists to book. However, laws and law-enforcing machinery can curb terrorism only to a certain extent. Certain other steps also need to be taken to effectively deal with this malady. For instance, cooperation of the general public is very essential. People should not panic. They should keep their heads cool and maintain communal harmony, as the objective of the terrorists is to bring about chaos in the country. Wherever possible, the terrorists try to incite communal hatred which may lead to a civil war so that they can overthrow the government.

The public should supplement the work of the police force by informing about any suspicious-looking object or shady-looking person moving about in a suspicious manner. Awareness among the public about the need to help the law-enforcing machinery goes a long way in tackling terrorism. The intellectuals of the country should come forward and denounce the terrorists from public platforms. Writers, journalists and poets should boldly write, condemning the acts of terrorism. This will inspire confidence and courage among the common man.

Religious leaders should also openly and clearly condemn terrorism. An appeal should go forth from temples, mosques, churches and gurudwaras against the acts of violence of the terrorists. The places of religion should not be allowed to be used by the terrorists. The moderate elements in the society should separate and assert themselves so that the extremist elements get isolated. Efforts should be made at the international level too. Several countries, today are threatened by the malady of terrorism.

Last but not the least, the government should sincerely look into the demands of the agitating sections. The reasonable and legal demands which can be fulfilled within the framework of the Constitution should be acceded to. This will prevent the agitationists from aligning themselves with the terrorists. The rulers should never act arbitrarily or dictatorially, for this is bound to lead to, sooner or later, militant resistance which is the first step towards terrorism. ●

16. Population Explosion

There has been an alarming increase in the population of India since the partition of the country. The massive increase in population can jeopardise the safety and security of the country and this increase is setting at naught all our plans and schemes. The existing population in India is not commensurate with its resources and overpopulation is surely an open invitation to poverty in a country where industry and agriculture are still backward. The need of the hour is that population should be regulated strictly in conformity with the available resources.

The increase in population can be attributed to the fall in death rate and the rise in life expectancy. Infant mortality has gone down due to the availability of better medical facilities. The rapidly increasing population has given birth to the twin problems of unemployment and food.

Various factors are responsible for the growing population. Poverty and ignorance leads to more and more children in the lower strata of the society. Moreover, in some rural areas, a man with many sons and grand sons is considered to be lucky. The birth of a girl in an Indian family is said to be a liability while the birth of a son is an occasion to be celebrated. Couples having only daughters may go on producing children year after year until they get a son who alone can bring them salvation or *moksha* by performing their last sites.

Early marriage among Indians makes the couples stay together at the most fertile period of their lives and this results into a team of children. The ignorant masses believe that every new child brings his own luck with him and the manual workers look upon the arrival of a male child as an addition to their earning capacity.

It is necessary to tackle the problem of over-population in the interest of the economic prosperity of all Indians. Family planning, whose object is to control the size of a family and to prevent the births of too many children, can play a useful role in this regard. Nothing should be left to chance and people should be made to realise that the need of planning a family is to have a better standard of living. Government hospitals and primary health centres should make a commendable contribution to family planning. Intensive propaganda should be done by the government to popularise the objects of family planning. Contraceptives — vasectomy, tubectomy, the use of loop in women, pills and condoms — should be encouraged.

As family planning alone cannot achieve spectacular results, obstacles in the way of family planning should be removed. The masses should be educated to have a pragmatic approach to life, as a part of the family planning programme. The age for marriage should be raised by law. Couples having more than two children should be taxed. Young men and women should be given incentives for remaining bachelors and spinsters for a considerable time and rewarded for producing less children. ●

17. Student Unrest

Student unrest, universal in nature, is not a phenomenon peculiar to our country. All over the world young men in general and students in particular manifest signs of restlessness. Unrest among students in India is evidenced by the strikes, agitations, processions, demonstrations, gheraos, arson and defiance of authority.

As a matter of fact, it is the unrest in the minds of men that has brought about revolutions in the world and has generated new ideas. As such unrest among students should be welcomed by teachers, parents and statesmen as it shows a progressive outlook. Hence, there is nothing dangerous about unrest.

However, it is regrettable that the unrest among students has assumed fearful proportions as they have become defiant and disobedient. Sometimes they go on strike because they have genuine grievances like poor facilities in colleges, insufficient furniture and equipment in class rooms and laboratories and incompetent staff to teach them. Sometimes they go on strike because one of their leaders has been fined for misconduct. Transfer of a particular teacher, detention of students, difficult question papers are the other excuses on which students resort to misbehaviour and begin to ventilate their grievances by indulging in rowdyism. They damage college buildings, destroy or hijack buses and even loot shops. Sometimes they have brushes with the police and when a student or two are injured as a result of police lathi-charge, the unrest assumes more serious proportions and it becomes a state wide affair.

Some educationists are of the view that the unrest among the students is a reflection of the general unrest in the country and the world. As India is passing through a great change and the old order is changing and the new is taking place, the modern student is an active observer of the changing events. He had expected that the dawn of independence would open up new opportunities for progress in life but he is disillusioned and unhappy to see that the leaders of the country are corrupt, politicians are dishonest and inefficient bureaucrats are thriving while their own future seems to be bleak and this state of affairs leads to student unrest. Some people blame the present education system for breeding unrest among the students. The current education system is aimless and does not provide any spiritual or moral training. Students, after taking degrees, fail to get jobs which leads to frustration.

Also, parents have become indifferent to their children and politicians use the students to further their own vested interests. Students become handy tools whenever the politicians want to protest against a particular policy of the government. Students, being young and volatile, follow the politicians blindly and resort to rampage. This does not however, mean that students should not be aware of the political developments in the country. But they must remember that their primary duty is to study.

Leaders and educationists should also understand that the problem of student unrest is psychological in character and requires a sympathetic solution. As the students of today are the leaders of tomorrow, it is incumbent upon the teachers, parents and politicians to direct their minds in the right direction. The students' energies should be channelised in the right direction and they should not be made victims of oppression, suppression and repression. The leaders of the country should set noble examples of conduct for the students to emulate. Also, they should be provided opportunities for creative expression of their energy. It is also the duty of the students to discipline themselves and of the government to keep the teachers contented by providing them handsome salaries and better status. ●

18. Life in a Big City

Life in most big cities is disgusting and we often hear people exclaiming that they are sick of the confined, cribbed and cabined life of big cities. Life artificial and completely cut off from Nature. Most romantic poets have desired to escape in the lap of Nature from this city life where in the glare of the neon tubes, man forgets the movement of the sun, the moon and the stars. William Cowper has correctly remarked "God made the country, and man made the town."

We cannot enjoy life while living in a big city as here it is deprived of real inner ecstasy in spite of the fact that most of the amenities of civilised life are readily available. City people have to work like slaves, according to fixed routines, as they are mad after the material comforts of life. Sometimes it may not be a rush for material comforts but even getting the bare minimum necessities make city people lose their peace of mind.

Most of city dwellers have pale faces and sunken eyes and they do not inhale fresh air as they live in congested areas which are further polluted by smoke, dust and grime. The sanitary conditions of some cities are extremely unsatisfactory. If there are palatial buildings in a city, there are dirty slums as well. City dwellers are selfish, greedy, cunning and crafty. They are not aware who their next-door neighbour is. They might dress well and have polished manners but many of them are selfish creatures who are devoid of the milk of human kindness. Most of them seem to be groaning under the weight of taxes and sex and they live a life of fever and fret, which makes them suffer from many diseases such as hypertension, heart ailments and diabetes.

Life in a big city is a strange blend of paradoxes. On one hand there are sky-scrapers and on the other, there are dirty hovels, and affluence and abject poverty exist side by side. Posh buildings and restaurants exist side by side with factories emanating smoke. The rich empty their pockets while shopping while the beggars give out heart-rending cries for alms.

No doubt, cities do have certain attractions which are not available in villages. This makes many people from villages flock to cities. Cities are centres of trade, commerce and industry and cities like Mumbai are full of glitter and glamour. One can have the best possible education in a city. Besides, there are cinema houses, gardens, public parks, zoos, museums, hotels and restaurants. Facilities such as well-equipped libraries, hospitals, dispensaries and specialised medical aid which are easily available in the cities and towns are conspicuous by their absence in villages. There are grand buildings, art galleries and exhibition ground halls in cities and a city dweller can keep himself busy even by window-shopping. Cities are also the centres of political activities.

To conclude we may say that life in a big city is a blend of joys and sorrows. It has advantages as well as disadvantages. If all the amenities of life are available in a city, evils like drinking pubs and gambling dens are also there. ●

19. Pollution

The word 'pollution' which literally means contamination or defilement is causing irrepairable loss to a city dweller. The clouds of pollution loom over the metropolitan cities of our country. The problem of pollution is being worsened each day due to uncontrolled migration from rural areas to cities, industrial units which are haphazardly located and vehicular traffic.

The air is polluted, the water is polluted and the noise we have to endure is assuming alarming proportions. All these pose a serious threat to the health of a city dweller who is suffering from serious ailments such as high blood pressure, respiratory diseases like asthma and skin-related disease. Children who live in the polluted environment

of the cities are the most unsuspecting and vulnerable victims of this menace.

Industries emanate carbon mono-oxide, sulphur dioxide and other poisonous gases and this poses a serious threat to the city dwellers. Untreated industrial waste pollutes the water of rivers which ultimately leads to water pollution. The ecosystem is disturbed due to the discharge of sewage and harbour water in the coastal waters. The silence of the atmosphere is disturbed by loud music from stereos, different type of vehicles and noise from the machinery and factories.

According to the World Commission on Environment and Development, the danger of pollution has become universal and without resolute steps in the right direction, the very future of mankind will be jeopardised. Extensive steps for eliminating pollution have been taken by the Indian government. The protection of the environment is now a major agenda of the government and about thirty major enactments. The Wildlife Protection Act, the Forest Conservation Act, the Air Act, the Environment Protection Act, the Motor Vehicle Act etc. are the most prominent of these. The Environment Protection Act, 1986, which is a landmark legislation, provides for the protection of the environment and also aims at plugging all the loopholes in other related Acts.

Efforts are also afoot to minimise pollution in grossly-populated areas of the country. Unleaded petrol is being provided in most of the states of India with the help of a Joint Action Plan of the Central Environment and Petroleum Ministries. Other measures to eliminate pollution include 'Eco-mark' label on the consumer products that are environ-friendly. Seventeen categories of heavily polluting industries have been identified by the Pollution Control Board which is the national apex body for assessing and monitoring the control of air and water pollution.

In order to make the pollution control programme a success, awareness must be created at the grassroots level otherwise in spite of the best efforts of the government and non-government agencies, much progress cannot be expected. If every individual takes upon himself the responsibility to ensure that he will keep his environment pollution-free, pollution can certainly be checked if not completely eliminated. ●

20 Fashions

A fashion may be defined as a mode or way or manner in which a thing is done or made. It implies a slight departure from the usual. In common parlance fashion means following the up-to-date cut and style in tailoring standards. Fashions are a special feature of the modern competitive society though they change every day and the rage of today becomes the ridicule of tomorrow.

It is said that fashions govern us like a tyrant who rules in a strict manner. Sometime it becomes very difficult for an average man to keep pace with changing fashions as they make exacting demands on our pockets. The west is the land of fashions and the ultra modern fashions come from the movie world of Hollywood. Paris is also said to be the centre of fashions where the French ladies are said to get their costumes stitched by the tailor and they hurry back to their homes to wear the newly stitched costumes. However, when they are on the thoroughfares of Paris, they find that the style and cut of their dress is out of fashion. People in India also imitate European fashions.

Fashion shows are held in big cities and tailors and fashion designers govern the world as fashions are dominating our day-to-day life. Young men and dandy young women like to wear fashionable dresses to be acclaimed and appreciated by others. College students — both boys and girls — pay maximum attention to their clothes as fashions are on the increase. A visit to the present day college will give the impression that ours is not a poor country but a land of actors and actresses.

Much of their time is spent in dressing up. Boys like to look smart and attractive in the presence of girl students and put on showy clothes, wear goggles and wear the dress which is trendy and in vogue. College girls outsmart boys in looking fashionable. Girls have a natural love for pretty dresses and in college they get an opportunity to manifest this love. Girls want to be admired and chased by boys and wear body-hugging dresses by which the contours of their bodies are displayed to the advantage of the male eye. Boys and girls want to look like some famous heroes or heroines of the movie-world and studies for many of them are merely a pastime. Fashion, no doubt, enhances the charms of a woman but acts as a great distraction to the male students.

Stephen Leacock has rightly said, "Men can't study when women are around". Fashions among students are confined not only to dresses. Seeing every movie that is released, visiting expensive restaurants and hotels, drinking the costliest whiskey or wine and smoking the costliest cigarettes are also part of fashions. Also, some students develop mannerisms like film actors and actresses and have the stories and songs of films at their finger tips but they are indifferent to the lessons taught in the class.

Some boys like to smoke in the style of movie actors forgetting that actors may be rolling in wealth whereas they will have yet to seek respectable jobs after coming out of the portals of college. Besides, they discuss films, cricket and whatever that catches their eye and are devoid of any spiritual or moral values.

Extravagant fashions have caused considerable harm to the student community and there has been a steep decline in the pass percentage in the university examinations.

Parents should check their wards from adopting extravagant fashions. Young men and women should be weaned away from this menace and they should be exhorted to follow the noble ideals of simple living. ●

21. Stress

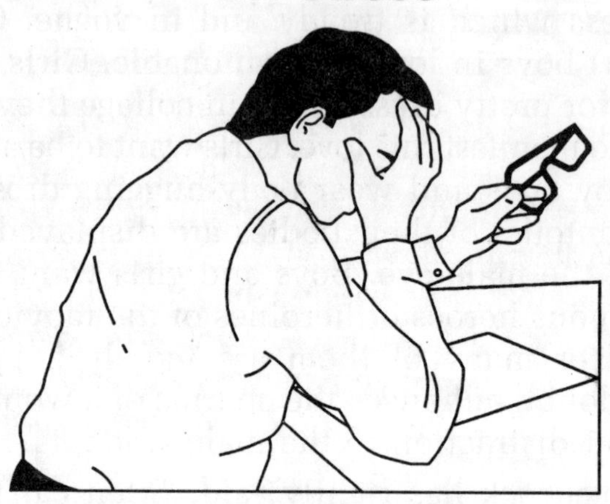

In today's world, possessing more and more things which money can buy has become a status symbol and money and prestige have become synonymous with each other. To earn more money and to outsmart our relations and acquaintances is a matter of prestige. Today every one strives for money, affluence and success and ambition is the buzzword. The result is that the man of today leads a fast-paced, competitive and stressed life.

Rat race for luxurious lifestyle is taking its toll by generating stress. Stress may be defined as pressure, anxiety syndrome, strain or tension. There is likely to be mental, emotional or physical stress if one is unable to cope with the hectic lifestyle. Man of today has a very high degree of commitment but the time available at his disposal is less and he is haunted by the fear that he is likely to be left behind and this fear inevitably leads to a lot of stressful situations.

Also, modern man leads a mechanical lifestyle which further aggravates strain. There is lack of physical exercise due to confinement to one's place of work for longer periods. Not having a balanced diet, lack of nutritious diet and consumption of more coffee, tea and alcohol also makes people more prone to stress. It is high time the modern man devises some method to overcome stress. Stress can be overcome to some extent if we follow a disciplined lifestyle and manage our time better. Also priorities should be given to those areas which need more attention. Taking breaks from hectic work can counter stress to some extent. Also, one is relieved of the monotony of daily life by taking regular holidays and visiting some new place, especially some hilly place; calm, serene and far-removed from the madding crowd of big cities, where one can rejuvenate one's heart and mind. Meditation, yoga and spiritual pursuits are also very useful to counter stress.

Stress can also be minimised if not completely eliminated, by doing regular exercise and controlling one's diet. Spending quality time with near and dear ones can also go a long way in controlling stress. ●

22. Corruption

There is no doubt that after independence, India has progressed in many areas. But it is also rightly said that the two factors which characterise the Central and State governments in our country are Minus efficiency and Plus corruption. If India has flourished in any sphere, that is corruption. India is in the grip of the worst form of corruption. Corruption in the country's public and administrative life has considerably increased during the last two decades. Corruption, to a certain degree, is a legacy of the British Raj and is not peculiar to India alone but is a universal phenomenon.

Official files and documents do not move unless the palms of the concerned officials are greased. One cannot get the official copy of a court judgement from the copying agency of the court unless one pays some extra money to the typist, besides paying the official court fees. An honest man's application is subjected to delays by red tapism. Corruption in some public-dealing offices has reached a saturation point and people have started taking corruption for granted. The lot of the common man is miserable as he has to stand in long queues, grease the palm of petty peons and clerks and put up with tyrannies all around whereas businessmen and industrialists are aware of the fact that they can get anything done by paying bribes. We all talk about corruption but the half-hearted measures taken to root out corruption are neutralised and turn out to be a futile exercise.

Our leaders do not seem to be keen on removing corruption and one gets the impression that these leaders themselves are responsible for the corruption in the country. Inquiry Commissions and Investigating Committees are merely an eye-wash as the ministers are not concerned with any real purpose served as such and the result is that corruption is eating into the vitals of our society. It seems extremely difficult to clean the Augean stables of corruption.

Some great statesmen and intellectuals have advocated that some eminent statesmen, with no political ambitions, should constitute themselves into a National Forum, should collect and process material regarding complaints, and prima facie cases can be established to publish their findings and press the government to appoint regular Commissions of inquiry.

Some persons have discounted the utility of *Lok Pal* and *Lok Ayukta* since they have become the greatest source of corruption and no body acts on their information because of their trade union spirit and the philosophy of "Touch one; touch all, therefore touch none". Most ministers spend large sums of money to win elections, which to most of them are investments to be recovered with compound interest. Politicians are, thus, far more liable to corruption.

The cure of corruption may lie in the appointment of a registrar of public grievances against the administration, who is appointed by the Parliament and who enjoyed great authority and whose main function should be to handle citizen's complaints against administrative abuse, incompetence and corruption. ●

23. Future of English in India

Ever since India became free, the English language controversy has been raging, though English enjoyed a privileged place in the educational set up of the country for about two centuries. Independence fostered the feeling of nationalism in every sphere of Indian life and the question of national language also cropped up.

After the British quit India, it was natural that the patriotic fervour of the people would assert itself in the form of antipathy for the English language. The continuance of English language in administration and educational institutions was questioned by the people, though the supporters also came out with their strong support and feelings of continuance of the language. This controversy escalated into polarity between North and South India and people started becoming violent in defence and in opposition to the English language.

In 1950, when India became a Republic, a compromise was made and English was allowed by the Constitution of India to continue for fifteen years. Even the first Prime Minister of Independent India, late Jawahar Lal Nehru said, "English is our major window on the modern world". During this period English was substituted by Hindi as the lingua-franca of India. However, it became necessary for the Parliament to pass the necessary legislation to continue the use of English language even after 1965. The government realised that India could not do without English for many years to come.

The passage of official language Amendment Bill in December 1967 reiterated this position and the three language formula — English, Hindi and Regional — has been widely accepted by all the states in the country and English continues to enjoy an important place in the educational institutions and many departments of the government and the reality has been accepted that English cannot be discarded lock, stock and barrel.

Most right-thinking persons hold the opinion that English constitutes a unifying force in the country, as according to them, united India is a land of vast diversities and the knowledge of English helps Indians in one part of the country to be understood in other parts of the country. People in the southern part of India in general and Tamil Nadu in particular are not very keen to study Hindi and they insist that English should not be discontinued at the university level. Also, the migration of students from one university to another will become difficult if there is a different medium of teaching in different universities.

It is only through the medium of English language that all the advance knowledge in different sciences and researches made in the fields of medicine is made available to Indian students. Keeping Indian students away from English would be keeping them away from the latest technological, scientific and other developments. Besides, English is an international language and the most widely understood in the world. English is the language of trade, commerce, diplomacy and has a very rich literature. Without English we would have been deprived of the wisdom of William Shakespeare, William Wordsworth, John Milton, Ruskin, Carlyle, Hazlitt, Bacon and Charles Lamb. It was through this language that Swami Ram Tirath and Vivekanand carried the message of India to the English people. People sometimes argue that those knowing English language became unpatriotic. There is no substance in this view as most of our front rank freedom fighters were educated in English.

English will continue to enjoy an important place in India as a good command over English is considered a passport to better employment in life. The number of public schools is increasing each day and more and more people, especially those who can afford, prefer to send their children to those schools where English is taught from the very beginning. The opponents of English hold the view that English is not our own language and it is a relic of slavery and a challenge to our patriotism. Besides, students find it difficult to express themselves in a foreign language and their talent remains hidden. Also, science and technology books can be read by only those few students who are well-versed in English.

If the books on science, technology and medicine are translated into Hindi and regional languages, all the students will not have to study English. There is no use thrusting English on unwilling students. The policy makers perhaps want to retain English because there is the consideration of the unity of the country in their minds. Therefore, a liberal approach is being made to the question of the proper place of English and it is being accommodated as one of the three languages in the three-language formula. Hindi is the official language of the Union and is expected to become, in due course, the lingua-franca of the country. English will continue to enjoy a high status so long as it remains the principal medium of education at the university stage and the language of administration at the Centre and in many of the States. Even after the regional language becomes the medium for higher education in the universities, a working knowledge of English will still be an asset for all students and a reasonable proficiency in the language will be essential for those who join college. Some would be needing a working knowledge of English or Hindi, while others would be requiring a greater proficiency in them. Though English is likely to remain the most important library language to be studied, a certain number of students would learn a library language other than English in more or less all parts of India. ●

24. Hobbies

A hobby can be defined as a pursuit which one undertakes in leisure for pleasure and not for profit. The hobby does not aim at earning any money, though sometimes it may indirectly bring about financial benefit. A man engaged in the collection of stamps may unknowingly collect a few rare stamps which may bring him money. Hobbies reflect the life and personality of a person and give us an insight into the temperaments, tastes and propensities of the people.

Life in the modern age has become monotonous, dreary and dull and hobbies provide the required change from the drudgery of a routine life and serve the purpose of a refreshing change. The fever and fret of our life is forgotten, though may be for a short-time, when one is engaged in a hobby.

Reading fiction and journals, stamp-collecting, coin-collecting, painting, fishing, photography, writing to pen friends are some of the popular hobbies. Collecting autographs of celebrities, boating, playing golf, cricket and other games are also the hobbies of some persons. Gardening is more or less confined to rural areas as there is hardly any place left for this hobby in the urban areas.

Hunting, which used to be a very popular hobby in the olden days, when means of entertainment were very few and far between, has been given up as it involved the killing of innocent animals.

Some of the popular hobbies among women are social-work, knitting, stitching, crochet-work though some women indulge in negative hobbies of rumour-mongering and scandle mongering.

As it is rightly said that an idle man's brain is the devil's workshop, one should not remain idle and hobbies should fill up one's leisure which can serve as a welcome interlude in the tedium of one's daily life. Recreation is not the only aim of hobbies which give us knowledge we don't get from text books. Besides serving as mental tonics hobbies are an excellent way of spending one's leisure.

One should pursue only those hobbies which are useful such as gardening, photography, riding, swimming, yachting as they enable us to use our leisure in a harmless way; while hobbies such as gambling, drinking and cards playing which do not promote real happiness, should be discarded. Besides scandal-mongering, character-assassination, rumour-mongering are very dangerous and can create many enemies for us.

People living in big cities often visit picnic spots and places in the lap of Nature to refresh themselves. It is disheartening that most people in our country do not use their leisure in a proper manner. There are some whose leisure is spent in an unplanned manner while there are others whose leisure is utilised in supplementing their meagre income. The life for the poor is a night-marish experience. Most of us waste our leisure in visiting friends and watching useless movies. It is also equally regrettable that some college students spend their leisure in watching cheap movies and reading pornographic fiction which corrupt their minds and deprive them of any useful pursuit.

There is no doubt that hobbies are the best means of spending leisure and useful hobbies can certainly keep people away from evil ways of life. They channelise the exuberance, enthusiasm and energy of the young and can go a long way in solving many complex problems. Hobby should not be converted into a dull dreary task but should be treated as a mental pastime. Regular work should not be ignored for the sake of a hobby. ●

25. A Happy Life

All persons want to be happy and all have their own conception of a happy life. Some think that they can be happy if they are able to get a lot of money. Others think that they will be happy if they have power over others and if they are considered as 'great men' by others. Still others' happiness lies in the company of beautiful women.

According to Henry Wotton, a happy life is free from flattery and worldliness. Happy is the man who does not fear death, who is not impulsive and who spends time in reading scriptures or in silent meditation. Such a person never hopes to rise in life nor does he fear to have a fall. According to Alexander Pope, real happiness can only be derived from solitude and a person who lives in solitude is a happy person. A person who has a few acres of land and whose needs and desires are met locally and who does not have the wander thirst is a happy man. A happy man enjoys good health, peace of mind and enjoys the ecstasy of study and meditation in turns and takes delight in innocent pleasure.

However, it is not possible for all of us to follow the above ideals of happiness. Some people can never think of leading the solitary life of a saint and hence they can never sever their ties with other human beings with whom they must associate, interact and have cordial relations. People, to be happy today, would like to have economic security — a well-paid job or some prosperous business. They do not believe in the philosophy of the blessings of poverty. A poor man's life is so miserable that it is not worth their envy. Some people do not wish to hoard money or possess a lot of black money but they believe that happiness lies in decent living. They do not want to be afflicted with penury, misery and wretchedness.

There is no doubt that the life of an idler cannot be a happy life. One must work hard to earn a decent living but one must have some leisure to stand and stare. A good heath also provides happiness and an unhealthy person cannot experience happiness. Good society and sincere friends with whom one can share one's joys and sorrows are also essential for happiness. It has been rightly said, "sorrow shared is sorrow halved." One should be open and above board in one's dealings with others since frankness and open-heartedness are necessary conditions for a happy life. Having sympathy for the weaker sections of society and less privileged, promoting the happiness of others, keeping away from selfishness and hard-heartedness also bring peace and happiness. ●

26. Value of Sports

The value of sports and games is recognised by all educationists today. Books develop our mind but games develop our body. A sound mind is always there in a sound body. This truth is universally acknowledged and accepted. Physical fitness, free from all ailments, is the desire of every human-being. Sports make our body stout and muscular. They fill the body with strength and vigour, they expand our lungs and increase the blood circulation. If one is physically fit, one feels happy and finds oneself capable of hard work. All forms of sport, cricket, football, volley ball, hockey, badminton, table tennis, rowing, swimming — entertain us and also provide the much-needed exercise. They are an excellent way to spend one's leisure time. In the play ground, one forgets the worries of the routine life.

Games and sports inculcate in us a spirit of sportsmanship, honesty, punctuality, regularity of habits. They also teach us the qualities of team spirit, leadership and obedience. They provide us a good training for playing the game of life in a sporting way. A true sportsman will not be sad at his defeat and not be overjoyed on his success. A true sportsman plays the game for the game's sake and not for winning always.

Each game is played under certain rules which are to be obeyed by all the players. Therefore sports teach us obedience and discipline and teach us the importance of cooperative efforts. They teach us how to command and how to obey. Above all, they encourage and develop the spirit of competition, a healthy spirit of rivalry and constantly lead to improvement in performance. Excess of games and sports may, however, make one neglect one's studies and regular work. ●

27. Technical and Vocational Training

The education system introduced in India by the Britishers has outlived its utility. It was introduced to

make us fit for white collar jobs. Technical and vocational training is the foremost need of the present day society. Purely literary education creates a dislike for manual labour. There are many ordinary graduates but no one needs them because a graduate is not fit for anything except general clerical work in an office. It is therefore essential that besides literary education, graduates should be given technical and vocational training.

Technical training will help us solve the problem of unemployment. It will prepare children for scientific and technical mode of social life. Vocational training keeps the body fit and helps in character building. It provides us a sense of the dignity of labour. Vocational or technical training is a good substitute for a hobby. We begin to realise that all work is noble and we begin to feel important that we are doing something worth-while for the society. It keeps us actively busy and we can have a good leisure for pleasure when we do some sort of vocational training.

Technical education provides a training of the head and hand and in a technical school, students use their hands and muscles to exercise their brains. And they observe with their eyes. Technical education will make the youth self-sufficient and will raise the standard of living. Also it will go a long way in solving the ever-growing problem of unemployment. ●

28. Purpose of Education

Education and human life are closely connected with each other. One has to acquire education so that human life becomes a complete whole. Education has four main aims. Firstly, education is needed to develop the personality of a student and to enable him to earn his bread. Secondly, education should enable him to play his role as a citizen in a democratic country. The third purpose of education is to inspire a student to develop all his hidden powers. The fourth aim is to build character of the individual or a student.

Population is increasing at a large scale in modern times and there are many unemployed youths. Therefore, today, education is a means to attain jobs. It is therefore an obligation of the country and the governments to make arrangements to give not only general education but technical and vocational training also. India is a democratic country. Democracy can not fully succeed unless its citizens are educated. If a proper system of education is not there, its citizens can be exploited by selfish politicians and business pirates.

Education helps a man to grow to his full stature. It enables him to develop his latent powers and faculties of nature. It helps him to develop his mental and spiritual powers. Education is the only tool for building the character of an individual. The first thing in which an individual is trained is social behaviour. Without education man cannot learn the art of living with others. A really educated person is a transformed individual. To him, the world becomes a bigger and more charming place. He is able to see more beauty and variety in the world. Unfortunately, character training and development of mental and spiritual potentialities are not given a proper place in the modern education system. The present system of education is just a passport to the boys for employment and to the girls for their marriages. Even our political world reflects a picture that education has not succeeded in its primary aim. ●

29. Dowry — A Curse

The custom of dowry has been prevalent in our society since times immemorial. The parents of the girls used to give certain items or money to the newly-wedded couples so that they could start a comfortable life. But the form of dowry has changed now-a-days. Today, the success of marriage is seen in terms of money and free gifts, not in terms of happy and conjugal relations.

The birth of a daughter in a Hindu family was considered as a sign of good luck. Now this birth is considered as a burden on the shoulders of the parents. Parents generally curse the day a daughter is born to them. In some far off rural and tribal areas, people are compelled to resort to homicide because of their poverty. These sinful acts are the shameful results of unwanted dowry system. If the girl child is spared to survive and grow, she becomes the neglected object of the house. Discrimination is made between daughters and sons and sons are preferred to daughters. Parents always remain worried about the marriage of their daughters.

The parents of the girls have to face huge demands of dowry when they go into the market in search of prospective bridegrooms. The demands of dowry are so high that their life-long savings seem a drop in the ocean. They have to borrow and are neck-deep in debt for ever. If the parents are unable to fulfil the demands of the groom's parents, the bride has to face many problems. She is rebuked, insulted and abused. The number of suicides among teenage brides is very high in the country.

Much has been said against dowry system but nothing has been done seriously. The government should start an aggressive campaign against dowry system. Government servants accepting dowry in cash or kind before or after marriage should be chargesheeted and terminated. It is a good step taken by the government that it has declared dowry a social crime and economic offence against humanity. This evil cannot be wiped out by laws and the steps taken by the government. The people must have an awareness and they should remove this evil from the society. ●

30. An Ideal Teacher

Teaching is the most respected profession even today when most of the professions have become commercial. The most respected person in one's life is a teacher. Parents give us birth and rear us but teachers make us real human beings. A good teacher is an incarnation of

God and he leaves an indelible impression on man's heart, mind and soul. The profession of a teacher continues to be honoured in spite of the fact that teaching is no more a service of God's people.

Teachers have started selling their services. They force the students to take tuitions after school hours. They charge very high tuition fees. Schools in big cities have become highly commercial. Many teachers exploit their profession as greed for money and position has entered this profession also.

But still there are a lot of teachers who are worthy of being worshipped. Every successful person has been fortunate to have availed the services of such teachers who continue to be the topic of students' discussions all their lives and they continue to get inspiration from them. India has produced teachers who have left indelible impressions in the hearts and minds of numerous students.

An ideal teacher should be sensitive, with a genuine ability to tune into the minds and feelings of the pupils. He should be tolerant towards his pupils because they are immature and in the process of learning. An ideal teacher should make even a boring lesson seem interesting and to enliven the atmosphere in the classroom. He or she should be capable of providing emotional support whenever needed. A teacher must be resilient, because teaching is a demanding profession that drains a person emotionally and mentally. A good teacher must be receptive to new ideas and alert to new changes. Last but not the least, an ideal teacher must practise what he or she preaches. He or she must live up to the standards he or she expects from the students. ●

31. Fear of Examinations

Examinations fill the examinees with fear because their future is fully dependent on them. The fear of examinations saps the courage and energy of the examinees. The bright students as well as dull tremble with fear the night before the examination. Some students prepare select questions and the brilliant ones are apprehensive of possible poor performance. They prepare all the questions and leave nothing to chance.

The fear of examination is unavoidable. The present system of examination is at fault to a great extent. This system is an age-old process and does not fully suit the present conditions. This system is not a genuine test of examinee's ability and calibre.

Even the dullest examinee can score the highest marks if he gets the question paper having the questions which he has fully crammed. A test of two or three hours may not sometimes, test the real talent or calibre of a student. Examinations should be a healthy process of testing one's ability and they should not be a fearful experience. Even many brilliant students weep a day before the examination. Success or failure is not entirely linked to the original intelligence and calibre of an examinee. Even a difference of a single mark may make or mar the future of an examinee.

The fear of examinations is going to live unless the pattern of examinations is changed to suit the present requirements. An alternative method of evaluating students' ability should be introduced. The present system of examinations is surrounded in controversy for a long time and needs the proper attention of the educationists. ●

32. Child Labour

Today, there are lakhs of children who work as wage-earners. They are deprived of childhood, love, nutrition and social association. Child labour emerged during the industrial revolution and today it has become a very serious problem. It is a world-wide phenomenon.

Extreme poverty, large families, lack of free and compulsory education and ignorance of parents are the most glaring causes of child labour. Children do not cause labour trouble and they are ready to accept lower wages. But sometimes, children are not paid for their labour and are kept as apprentices. Children from four years of age to fifteen years are made to work in glass factories, carpet industry, fire-cracker factories and they are paid as low as rupees five to eight for working for more than twelve hours daily. These children are not allowed to have contact with the outside world.

These children have no chance to attend school and have no choice except to work as unskilled labour. These children are compelled to live below poverty line all their lives. There are many laws against child labour in India and in other countries but these laws alone cannot control the exploitation of children. We must get the support of all the people of the society to control this menace.

According to the law, no child below the age of fourteen can be employed in any hazardous job. Another law states that children should not be made to work beyond their capacity and they should be given opportunities and facilities to develop in a healthy manner. However, all these laws have failed to check the problem of child labour. Stringent laws should be enacted and exemplary punishment should be given to those who exploit children for their selfish ends. ●

33. The Festival of Holi

India is a land of festivals and many festivals are celebrated here. Holi is one of them. It is, in fact, a festival of colours. A night before Holi, a bonfire is lit. There is a religious background to this. King Hiranyakashyap tried to burn his son, Prahlad who used to worship Lord Vishnu. The king's sister Holika had a blessing that she could not be burnt in fire. So the king asked his sister to help burn Prahlad. She sat in fire with Prahlad in her lap. But instead of Prahlad, Holika was burnt. Therefore Holi is burnt one day before to symbolise the victory of good over evil.

Some people say that Holi is celebrated in honour of Lord Krishna who killed a cruel demon on this day and filled the lives of people with joy. Holi is celebrated in all villages, towns and cities. People sing folk songs and dance to the beat of drums. Children as well as adults celebrate Holi with great enthusiasm. People smear 'gulal' on each other's forehead. The children get ready with syringes and buckets full of coloured water. They throw it on friends, relatives and even passersby. Some throw water-balloons. As the balloons hit like missiles, their sale is banned during the Holi festival.

Feasts are enjoyed and delicacies are served. Some people drink excessive alcohol on this day. Some people spoil this festival by gambling and playing Holi with grease and dirty colours. Holi should be celebrated in the true spirit as it is the festival of joy and celebrations. ●

34. Co-education

Coeducation means that there should not be separate schools and colleges for boys and girls. There has been a controversy on the subject of co-education. Those who support co-education say that this system has proved to be a success in the western countries where it was introduced many years ago. According to them, this system is economical and in coeducation there is a free exchange of ideas between boys and girls. The presence of girls among boys in the same schools and colleges will lead to healthy interaction between the two sexes.

Those who oppose this system say that there are no benefits as it corrupts the minds of both boys and girls. Moreover, giving the same type of education to both boys and girls is against Nature.

In big cities most of the public and convent schools are coeducational. It has been observed that co-education is a more healthy process. Students passing out of co-educational schools and colleges are fully confident of themselves. They have no inhibitions for each other. Co-education has resulted in a healthy atmosphere in offices and other places of work. The seeds of this healthy process are sown in co-educational schools and colleges. Women are becoming more confident and are seen working with men in more or less all fields. Women are no longer the commodities which were involved only in the house-hold work. It is therefore safe to conclude that co-education system has come to stay. ●

35. My Pet Dog

A pet provides a great joy in one's life. My pet dog Sheru is a source of pleasure as well as of security and protection. Dog has been in man's service since times immemorial and no other animal is as sincere and as faithful as the dog. My pet, Sheru is not a status symbol for me but a necessity. I got Sheru two years back when it was a small puppy of three months. Sheru was gifted to me by my uncle who was tranferred to other station. Now, I cannot think of life without Sheru.

Sheru is an Alsatian. Sheru is of medium height, has a curved bushy tail, shining eyes and strong jaws. It has been trained fully. It is quite strong and its doggie habits are wonderful. It has wonderful toilet habits. It makes a strange sound when it wants to go for a walk. Sheru stands, runs and fetches things as he is commanded and is the envy of many dog owners. Sheru can be seen around our house most of the time. It is generally calm and gentle but it starts barking fiercely at the approach of strangers. It recognises the persons who visit our home regularly and does not bark at them. It obeys the commands and does not disturb us unnecessarily. It never jumps on sofas or beds and does not poke his nose when we are eating our meals.

My Sheru is vegetarian as he is not given meat but milk, bread, biscuits, etc. I take him out for long walks every morning and evening. Sheru provides me great company and we even play together with a ball. I am proud of Sheru. ●

36. Cinema

Cinema is one of the most wonderful inventions of modern science. It is the most popular form of entertainment. People belonging to all strata of society enjoy seeing cinema. The aim is only entertainment. However, cinema is a great means and media of education, promoting business and trade, bringing cultures closer and cultivating healthy atmosphere. It also helps in establishing strong social ties and removing the caste enmity and creating an atmosphere of fellow-feeling. Cinema is a cheap means of recreation and social reformation.

However, most of the films produced in the modern times lay stress on easy and dizzy life. They do not portray values of honesty, hard work and public well being. Film goers imbibe negative traits in their personality such as beating, cheating, robbing and indulging in other anti-social and inhuman activities. Most of the films now, deal with sex, crime and violence. These films are responsible for the increasing number of thefts, murders and rapes in the world.

Late night shows are full of poor labourers, rickshaw-pullers, coolies and other daily wage earners who have no time during the day as they have to work to earn a living. Matinee shows are watched by the students who feel better at cinema halls than at schools and colleges. Parents are generally not aware of the whereabouts of their children.

But cinema has got a great educative value. The documentary films on art, science and history give first-hand knowledge to the uneducated masses. Cinema is an effective means of propaganda against prevailing social customs and systems. Historical films can promote our culture to new horizons and heights.

According to the opinion of certain people and critics, cinema is more disadvantageous than being advantageous. Vandalism, goondaism, rapes, thefts, murders and dacoities take place after an evil person has seen a film. The cheap popular films leave a bad influence on the impressionable minds of boys and girls. Stories depicting indecent scenes of love and passion quite far away from the real life mar the character of the young boys and girls and should not be screened. Cinema can uplift the society in all the fields but caution is needed so that it does not become a curse. ●

37. Students and Politics

It has been a controversial topic for a long time whether students should actively participate in politics or not. Some politicians, teachers and students are of the view that students should whole-heartedly participate in politics and take active interest. Those who are against this view also strongly put forward their points.

Some people believe that politics, being a dirty game, creates groups and parties among the students. This leads to a lasting rivalry among them and disturbs their peace of mind thereby harming their academic progress. Students in schools and colleges should not waste their time in party bickerings as their main duty is to study. Students should not be involved in political tussle with each other. By doing so, we don't do justice with them. They participate in strikes, demonstrations and processions. At times there is a clash with the police or college authorities and students are put behind bars and have to contest legal cases in the court. Thus very valuable time is lost if students participate in politics. Many innocent students who really want to study, also lose their valuable time by associating with those who are actively involved in politics. In short, participation in politics spoils the career of a student and renders him useless for the rest of his life.

Those who favour students' participation in politics say that education means all-round development and not only acquiring literacy. Participation in politics leads to the all-round development of an individual student. The student comes to know of what is happening in the country and the world around him. He does not remain a mere book-worm but learns the qualities of leadership and he becomes aggressive, dominating and an alert young man ready to face the battle of life after college. Participation in politics makes him a good citizen, a responsible person and a cultured human being. He gains a fair practice of debating and putting forward his view point with force and conviction. He acquires the qualities of leadership and develops the qualities of courage, sincerity of purpose, spirit of service, self-discipline and devotion to duty. Such people are of the view that the great leaders of our nation were great student leaders in their student life.

We can conclude that students should tread the middle path. Students should not involve themselves very actively in politics which is sure to harm their studies, the main goal of student life. ●

38. A Pilgrimage to a Holy Place

People belonging to different faiths and religions want to go on their pilgrimages again and again. The Hindus, the Sikhs, the Muslims and the Christians all go to their holy places. Some of the important places of pilgrimage of the Hindus are — Vaishno Devi, Jwalaji, Shri Badri Nath, Haridwar, Pushkar, Prayag Raj, etc. The Muslims have Ajmer Sharif, Mecca, Madina etc. The Christians also have their own places of religious importance. Since times immemorial, people undertake arduous journeys to pay their obeisance to God.

In temples worshipping is done and many religious fairs are held. At Haridwar, fairs are held on the auspicious dates of the year. Worshipping is also done in the rivers like the Ganges at Haridwar. The Kumbha Fair is held after each twelve years. As several lakhs people come to take bath in the holy river Ganga, extensive arrangements are made by the authorities. According to the Hindus, the Ganga is a holy river and if a man takes a dip in this river on the auspicious occasion of Kumbha, his sins are washed away and he can achieve salvation.

Also, the Hindus immerse the ashes of the dead in the Ganga, at *Har-ki-paudi* so that the dead can get Heaven. People visit temples, offer prayers and carry the holy water of the Ganga to their homes. This pious water is used at the time of any religious ceremony. In the evening, the pilgrims throng at the 'ghats' to enjoy the beauty of the 'Aarti' of the Ganga. It presents a beautiful sight and is not only for the sake of beauty but for religious sentiments.

Apart from the religious sentiment, a bath in the cold water of the Ganga is very refreshing. The water contains medicinal properties and cures many ailments. This water does not get contaminated even if it is kept in water bottles for a very long period. Thus, for the Hindus, Haridwar is a very important place. Because of its piety and sacredness, the Rishis, Sadhus and other great saints have given a great importance to Haridwar. ●

39. Jawahar Lal Nehru

Pandit Jawahar Lal Nehru, the son of Pandit Moti Lal Nehru, was the first Prime Minister of independent India. For possessing the qualities of head, heart and soul, Jawahar Lal Nehru was greatly loved by Mahatma Gandhi, the father of the nation. Nehru was born on 14th November, 1889 at Allahabad in an aristocratic family. Nehru's father, Pandit Moti Lal Nehru was a distinguished lawyer of his time. He sent Jawahar Lal Nehru to England for higher studies, who passed out from Harrow School and Cambridge University. Nehru was brought up in the highest living standards of his time. He joined politics and became a devoted disciple of Mahatma Gandhi. Nehru started taking active part in the Indian freedom struggle and was sent to jail many times. He married Kamla Nehru in 1916. She also joined him in India's struggle for freedom. Jawahar Lal Nehru was a philosopher, writer, orator, statesman and politician. He has authored 'Discovery of India' and 'Glimpses of World History'. His oration and style of writing is grand and unparalleled.

Soon after Nehru joined the freedom struggle, he was recognised by all as a great leader possessing wonderful qualities and abilities. Indians and the Britishers reposed their faith in Nehru and even before India was free, he headed the first Interim Government formed by Indian National Congress in 1946. Earlier he was the President of Indian National Congress for four terms.

Under the patronage of Mahatma Gandhi, Jawaharlal Nehru was made the first Prime Minister of independent India. He took over from the British and was the first Prime Minister to hoist the flag of independent India from the ramparts of the Red Fort in Delhi on 15th August, 1947 at 12 midnight.

Jawahar Lal Nehru worked day and night to firmly lay the foundations of independent India. His contribution was so great that he is rightly called the architect of modern India. In order to build the infrastructure of free India, he earnestly sought help of all the friendly countries of the world. He started with the Five-year Plan which turned out to be a great success. He was the real king and benefactor of India. Under Nehru's prime ministership and dynamic leadership, India got a very high name and prestige in the community of the world.

Nehru became leader of the world politics and advocated Panch Sheel. Nehru left for his heavenly abode on 27th May, 1964 and left a void which is yet to fill. The whole world mourned his death and India has not since produced a leader of his ability, capability and calibre.

40. Rabindra Nath Tagore

Rabindra Nath Tagore was born on 6th May, 1861 in a well-to-do family of Thakurs in Bengal. He was looked after by his father as his mother passed away when Tagore was very young. From the very beginning Rabindra

Nath was averse to studying at conventional schools as according to him, the schools of his times were monotonous and adhered to set rules. He craved for the freedom of body and soul. He was allowed to receive education at home. He wanted to be carefree, dreamy and thoughtful. His love for Nature started growing with the passage of time.

He was sent to England when he was sixteen years old but he came back to India without doing anything. At the early age of fifteen he had started writing poetry and soon his poems were recognised and brought him name and fame. His poems reflected his thoughts and feelings. His early poems were given the title of "Morning Songs".

Tagore was a friend of all the humanity and a great patriot of the world. He spoke against narrow nationalistic ideas. He fought against the British rule in India though he was a great friend of the English for their qualities of discipline and statemenship. Tagore was a great genius who revealed to the Western world the greatness of India's past and her culture. He left a deep and indelible impression on everything around him. He was a great artist, who with equal force wrote poetry, drama, stories and painted pictures and performed music shows. His philosophic way of life won him great fame in India and the world.

Tagore was an authority on ethics and he delivered lectures extempore on any topic or occasion. "Geetanjali", Tagore's book in Bengali poetry, won him the Nobel Prize for literature. This prize is the first of its kind given to any Indian. Tagore's school at Shantiniketan won him international fame. This was a new system of education which emphasised working in close association with Nature, working manually and seeking Nature's benevolence. Tagore wanted to make this school a model of the old Indian tradition of "Gurukul". Ravindra Nath Tagore was awarded knighthood for his service to literature and art. However, in order to protest against the British rule in India, Tagore resigned it. Tagore died in 1941. ●

41. Mahatma Gandhi

Mahatma Gandhi, father of the nation was born on 2nd October 1869, at Porbandar, in Kathiawar, Gujarat. Mahatma Gandhi, also known as 'Bapu', was the greatest freedom fighter who got India freed from the British yoke. Gandhi's father was the Dewan of Rajkot and Bikaner and was a great nationalist of his time.

Mahatma Gandhi passed his matriculation in 1887 and went to England to study law and returned to India as a barrister. After that he went to South Africa to follow a law case. Gandhiji was shocked and pained to see the deplorable condition of Indians there at the hands of the foreign rulers. He was greatly moved and his love for the depressed and the neglected promoted him to initiate a movement against this oppression. Gandhiji's devout path against oppression through non-violent methods soon became very popular. On his return to

India in 1913, Gandhi started taking active part in the movement against the British Rule and joined the Indian National Congress.

Gandhiji initiated all non-violent means to fight the foreign rulers and thus gave a new shape to the freedom movement. Gandhiji led four Civil Disobedience Movements and was jailed many times. He became a very popular leader of the masses. He looked into the sorrows and problems of the lowest of the low, farmers, workers and the untouchables, as they were called. Gandhiji called the untouchables "Harijans" or the men of God. His approach was quite novel and effective as he succeeded considerably to rid the downtroddens of the fear of the land-lord, police and the money-lender.

Gandhi was a staunch Indian, a Hindu, a believer of the principle, "Work is Worship", as ordained in the great Indian classic, "Bhagwad Gita". He introduced the concept of 'Basic Education' which emphasised earning with learning. His work with the "Charkha" or the spinning wheel effected a revolution in the minds of the people. He also stressed that people should have freedom from poverty along with political freedom.

Gandhiji proved to the world that the weapon of non-violence was the strongest ever weapon to fight against the mightiest of the might. The mighty British power had to yield before Gandhi whom they found a force to reckon with. The British had to finally quit and India became independent in 1947. Gandhi was pained to see India dividing into two countries and wanted India to unite again but before his dream could come true, he fell to the bullets of Nathu Ram Godse on 30th January, 1948. ●

42. Future of Democracy

Democracy has been defined as the government of the people, by the people and for the people. This type of government was set up in India after independence. India is the largest democracy in the world. Every attempt has been made to strengthen democracy. Even then its functioning has not been very encouraging and some people have started doubting the future of democracy.

After setting up the democratic form of government, people thought that India would become a paradise and the country would regain its past glory. Unemployment, disease, poverty and starvation would be eliminated lock, stock and barrel. They hoped that the democratic form of government after independence would usher in 'Ram Rajya' in which every body would be happy. Unfortunately, the hopes of people have been belied. Fifty seven years after independence, sixty per cent of the people in India live below poverty line. Rising prices, corrupt and inefficient government machinery have made the life of the poor people a nightmare. We hear of starvation deaths in certain parts of the country. We hear of people feeding on garbage in other parts of the country. Also, we hear of people looting railway wagons and trucks carrying food grains.

No government after independence has been able to relieve the miseries of the common man. The leaders of democracy must hang their heads in shame as they have brought the country to economic ruin. People have lost their faith in democracy and they freely say that ministers, legislators, bureaucrats, inspectors and clerks are looting the country and there is no one to check them.

There are several reasons for which people of India have got disillusioned with the functioning of democracy. Many illiterate people do not know for whom to cast their vote. They vote for a person who either bribes them or who belongs to their caste or religion. Soon after independence, many new departments of the government were set up and they have become dens of corruption. Some misguided persons are of the view that in a democracy, one is free to do whatever one likes. The result is chaos, mal-administration, regionalism and provincialism. People have forgotten the country and they place their own interests above those of the country.

The functioning of democracy in India has not been very successful. Our successive governments have been characterised by two factors — minus efficiency and plus corruption. The common man is utterly disillusioned. There is complete lack of honest leadership. Promises of many leaders to bring in socialism have proved false. One wonders how the administration of this most corrupt democracy is running. May be it is the best form of government for those ministers who are ruling and looting the country. We need some very honest leaders who can revitalise the decaying and crumbling edifice of Indian democracy which is stinking with political opportunism, corruption, bungling and many other evils. ●

43. Beauties of Nature

Nature is the handiwork of God, just as art and industry are the creations of man. However, Nature surpasses in beauty all the handiworks of man. The beauty of Nature is one of the greatest benedictions which God has showered on mankind. Since times immemorial, poets and writers have waxed eloquent over the beauty of Nature. The modern industrial civilisation has, no doubt, made heavy inroads on the haunts of Nature, yet it remains a thing of beauty and a joy forever. Nature has always been a source of inspiration to the poets and

artists. William Words worth who is the high priest of Nature, believes that a visit to a mountains and lakes is equal to the visit to the church. To John Masefield, the call of the sea is irresistible. Shelley looks on the West Wind as destroyer and preserver. Byron looks upon the ocean as an image of God. Shakespeare finds sermons in stones, tongues in trees and books in running brooks.

The beauties of Nature offer a rich feast of delight to the eyes and ears of man. The crimson sun-rise, the glowing sun-set, the bright moon, the twinkling stars, the crystalling streams looking limpid like sapphire, the snow-capped mountains — all these beauties of Nature are indeed fascinating. The flora and fauna, the chirping birds also enhance the beauty of Nature. It is a pity that the modern man has no touch with Nature. He has sold his heart to the sordid boon of commercialism. He has come to believe in ledger philosophy based on calculation of profit and loss. Wordsworth rightly laments that 'the world is too much with us'. The modern man is completely alienated from Nature. The sea bathed in the moon light and the gentle howling winds do not appeal to him.

Nature is beautiful everywhere but there are occasions when even nature is red in tooth and claw. When the sea is rough and storms are blowing, a boatman on the high seas has to fight against the fury of Nature to reach a place of safety. But by and large Nature offers us many beauties. The star-spangled sky, the floating clouds, the multi-coloured rainbow, shining dew drops, butterflies flitting from flower to flower; glow worms shedding light — all give us beauty and joy.

Wordsworth feels that Nature is man's guide, friend and philosopher. If a man is in the throes of depression, the delightful scenes of Nature can enliven his spirit and make him cheerful. Beauties of nature are strewn everywhere, they are always fresh and they never become old or stale. Nature is the link between man and God. ●

44. The Choice of a Profession or Career You Shall Like to Choose

In olden days, choosing a profession was no problem when a son could easily adopt his ancestral profession. However, choice of a suitable profession is a problem these days when so many qualified persons are without jobs. An Indian student is like a rolling stone gathering no moss. He goes on drifting from one profession to the other profession without any definite aim before him. The choice of a profession is a hard nut to crack, though it is a vital decision for, the whole future happiness and prosperity of individual depend on it.

One should not choose a profession thoughtlessly and without proper planning. A young man should proceed with caution and care in choosing a profession. There are many professions open to an intelligent and hard-working person. Without hardwork and intelligence, success is not possible in any profession. I too am seriously thinking of a career for myself. I know that the choice of a profession depends on my taste and temperament. It is difficult to make a choice but one can have preferences. One can think of a number of professions such as Administrative Services, business, law, politics, business administration, engineering, medicine, teaching etc.

I don't like to enter Administrative Services because the officers have to play a second fiddle to illiterate ministers. Business offers many opportunities to earn money but businessmen have no rest from work. They remain busy making money. Law holds no attraction for me. Gandhiji rightly remarked : "Lawyers are liars". Legal profession does not suit men of honesty who do not like to compromise their principles. Moreover, an ordinary lawyer can not make even both ends meet. Lawyers of long standing, no doubt, make money but a fresher has no future in this line.

So far as medicine is concerned, it is purely a matter of having special skill in this line. Engineers are more machines than human beings. Politics, though quite a lucrative profession promises little to a man of character and morality. It is meant for the rich who have plenty of money and time to waste in electioneering and politicking and who are devoid of scruples. I don't like to enter government service. I am an independent-minded individual and cannot submit myself to the rigours of discipline of a government job. I don't wish to enter the Defence services of the country as I have no aptitude for the fighting profession. I cannot subject myself to the rigours of military discipline.

I think that I am cut for college lecturership. I am putting in all my efforts in preparing myself for lecturership in English language and literature. I am very fond of reading English literature, poetry, fiction, drama, biography etc. Shakespeare, Milton, Keats, Shelley and

English prose writers are my passion. I shall therefore be very happy to become a lecturer in English. The dignity and leisure of a lecturer's life are great advantages.

A college teacher cultivates cheerfulness and contentment. He has no financial worries or business worries. Moreover, a lecturer leads an honest life. There are no opportunities in his way to be corrupt. I shall endeavour to be a good teacher and a true friend, philosopher and guide to the young students. ●

45. Hostel Life

Hostel life is a very ideal life. It is a free and sacred life. In the hostel, the atmosphere is very congenial for studies and one develops qualities of cooperation, fellow-feeling and self-managing of affairs. If students take hostel life seriously, they can incalculate all the traits of a good citizen. A student can fully concentrate on studies in a hostel, as he is away from general worries and cares of life. Besides, he can participate in social activities and can learn virtues of head and heart from his senior students.

One can enhance one's knowledge while in the hostel. He can remove his weaknesses and become polished and cultured. He is able to shun his shyness and learns to speak fluently and expresses his ideas with confidence. By mixing up with different types of students, one learns to behave in a society and acquires good manners thereby sowing the seed of becoming a disciplined and good citizen.

There is no doubt that life in a hostel is full of responsibilities. One is free from the sharp eye of one's parents but here one has to use his own wisdom and intellect. Here one is one's own supervisor. This is the real test of one's self control and true self. One can fall an easy prey to evil habits, bad company, drugs, smoking and wasting of time. Here one can make or mar his career. A student in a hostel has no care except to devote all energies to studies. Hostel life gives all opportunities to a good student to make use of every thing — all facilities at hand, good teachers, good library, laboratory etc. The evil will automatically vanish, if a student can put his energies to the best use. Here one can shine like a jewel. However, if a student follows the negative track and evil ways, their grip will be tightened slowly and then it will be impossible for him to come out of the whole mess. In fact, hostel life is a memorable period of one's life. It gives one permanent friends and memories. It makes one self-confident, takes one out of parental care and teaches all the pros and cons of the reality of our life. ●

46. The Life of a Soldier

The life of a soldier is very hard, yet adventurous, far removed from selfishness, a life always demanding a sacrifice. A soldier is a great benefactor of the country and her citizens. Countrymen enjoy their peace because the soldier guards their boundaries and protects them from any aggression from the enemy forces.

The countrymen and the country as a whole go on their developmental work because there is peace and this peace can be ensured to the countrymen by the sincere and dedicated efforts of a soldier who is always guarding our borders. When war breaks out, all country-men are called up to do their duty to the nation.

Nelson said about his country, "England expects every Englishman to do his duty". Same is true of all the countries. The Indian Prime Minister, Late Lal Bahadur Shastri who recognised the importance of a soldier coined the slogan, "Jai Jawan, Jai Kisan", during the war with Pakistan in 1965. Shastri was able to realise the contribution of the soldiers by giving this slogan to the nation. As a farmer produces our food without which we cannot survive, a soldier protects us from both external and internal strife.

All the countrymen should have a great regard for the soldiers since they are the real friends of the nation. A soldier writes the destiny of the country with his blood. We can never forget the supreme sacrifice made by our soldiers in the wars with China and Pakistan. Getting back every inch of Indian land from the occupation of Pakistan in Kargil war is a story of great sacrifice and supreme heroism.

A soldier's life is very hard. He obeys all commands of his superiors and is ever ready to perform any duty and at any place — whether it is in the sea , air, water or at a very high altitude. He is the watchdog of the nation. Lord Tennyson has summed up the life of a soldier in his most memorable poem, the Charge of the Light Brigade :

Theirs' not to make reply,
Theirs' not to reason why,
Theirs' but to do and die. ●

47. My Best Friend

Man, by instinct, wants companionship as man is a social animal. Man meets numerous people in his journey through life but he does not make friends with all of them. This so happens because the essential condition of friendship is that there should be affinity of temperament, tastes and mind. Only the few in whom man discovers this affinity, he considers worth making friends with and such persons make a lasting niche in our life.

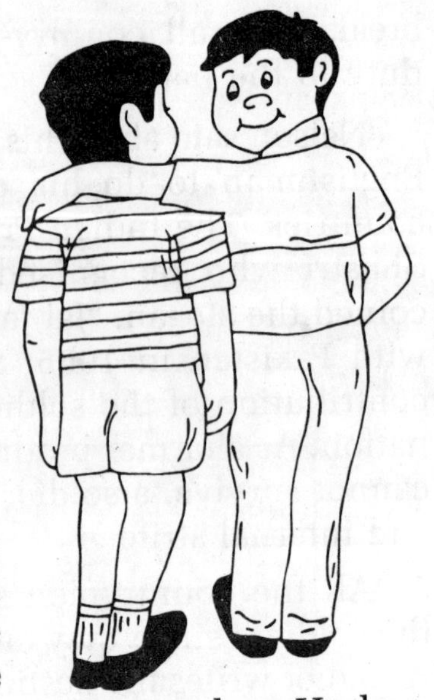

Monu is my best friend. He has a charming personality and bears a good moral character. He possesses pleasing manners. He father is a doctor and his mother is a teacher. He has been brought up in a congenial and healthy environment. Monu is a very obedient boy both to his parents and teachers. He respects all the elderly people and loves those who are younger to him. As he is the only child of his parents, he receives love from all. We play together, study together and enjoy each other's company.

He stands first in his class and all the teachers love him and admire him for his abilities. He has a very strong command over spoken and written English. He is a fine orator and can speak on any topic extempore. He has won many prizes in debates and essay competitions.

He plays football and is the captain of our school football team. He also goes for morning walks. He gets up early in the morning and devotes his time to studies. He also meditates and does yoga. He enjoys complete peace of mind.

Monu is God-fearing and does not hurt anyone's feelings. He has a soft corner even for the animals and birds. He is the lover of Nature and has written a few poems on Nature. These poems have been admired by one and all.

He is sincere in all matters and helps me whenever I need his help. I am proud of Monu and wants to follow his footsteps in all fields. I pray to God that our friendship should be enduring and should last for ever. ●

48. A Street Hawker

Street hawkers are a common feature of a city life. They can be seen in every street of a city. Street hawkers belong to a poor section of the city's population. They cannot afford to rent a shop and therefore they sell their goods in the streets. The hawkers are found selling vegetables, fruit and other wares of daily use. They start selling with shouts since morning. They carry the items either on their heads or in a cycle-cart. The housewives who cannot afford to go to the distant market buy vegetables and other items from these street hawkers.

A street hawker's way of selling goods is charming. He cries his ware and shouts in the street in an interesting tone. Some hawkers ring bells, some make strange sounds, some sing songs in order to attract the attention of their customers. His customers are housewives who buy vegetables, fruits etc. from him and children who buy ice-cream, sweets, toys etc. A street hawker caters to the need of the people and supplies them goods of their requirement at their doorstep.

As a street hawker has no fixed price, people bargain with him. Some street hawkers are not clean and do not cover their eatables. We should not buy eatables from such hawkers. Some of them are hardly able to make both ends meet. They have to work the whole day to earn their daily bread and feed their family. ●

49. A Visit to a Historical Place

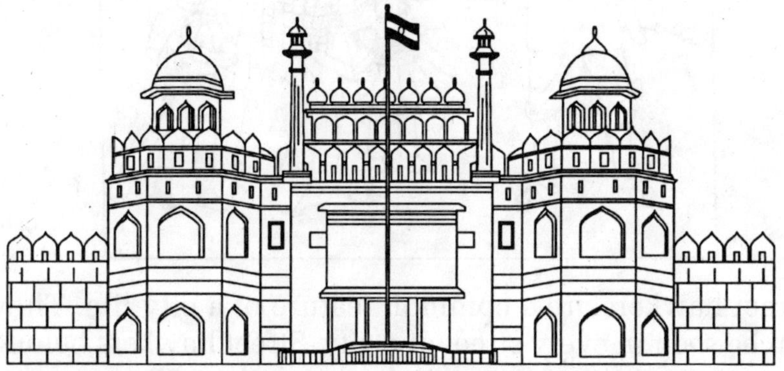

There are many historical places in India. These historical places are of much educational and historical value and hence it is essential that some of them should be visited by all the students.

The places of great historical value in Delhi are — Qutab Minar, Red Fort, Humayun's Tomb etc. One must visit these places, specially the Red Fort and the Qutab Minar. Last Sunday, the Principal of our school arranged a trip for the senior students to visit the Red Fort. Most of the students had already visited Red Fort but they desired to see it again.

We all reached our school at eight a.m. to join the trip. We went to the Red Fort by a specially hired bus. We reached Red Fort at nine in the morning and our History teacher, who was in-charge of the trip bought tickets for all of us. We then entered the Red Fort through the main entrance.

Along the entrance two rows of shops selling various objects of art besides selling handicrafts. During the Mughal times, this was known as Meena Bazaar. In this bazaar the princesses and the queens of the harem made their purchases. After crossing the lawn, we reached another gate where our tickets were checked. This building is known as 'Naubat Khana'. It was called Royal Drum House where Royal musicians used to play music five times a day in the Mughal times.

Then we saw 'Diwan-e-Aam' or the Hall of Public Audience. It has a marble dias and a marble canopy. The Mughal Emperor sat here and received the ministers, courtiers and other persons who came to meet him on official or public functions. The Prime Minister of the Mughal Emperor sat on the dias and the Emperor sat under the canopy on his throne. During those times, the walls of Diwan-e-Am were covered with paintings and it was decorated with precious stones. However, these valuable treasures are missing. Even the humblest citizen could come to Diwan-e-Am and present his petition to the king if he had any complaint against any body. Then we went to the 'Rang Mahal' which was a palace of pleasures and richly inlaid with precious stones in the Mughal period. In the centre of the hall ran a canal of refreshing water. It was known as the 'Nahar-i-Bihist'. In the middle of the hall, a fountain shaped like a flower played.

There is a 'Khas Mahal' beside the Rang Mahal. It has a beautiful marble screen. A scale is curved on the screen, depicting rigid justice which reigned supreme during the Mughal times. Then we went to the 'Diwan-e-Khas', the Hall of Private Audience where only select persons could meet the king such as ministers, princes, princesses and queens. Here was written the Persian couplet which means :

"If there be paradise on earth,
It is here, it is here, it is here".

The Red Fort also has the War Memorial Museum where weapons used in the First World War are exhibited. Here was the famous Peacock Throne and the Kohinoor diamond which was removed and taken to Iran by Nadir Shah. The throne was dismantled and broken into pieces. The Kohinoor diamond can now be seen in the British Crown.

50. Flattery

Flattery lies in tickling or humouring another man's vanity. Every body is proud of one thing or the other. Snobs and boastful persons want that others should praise them as they have a very high opinion about themselves.

Sometimes, the art of flattery proves to be a great asset in one's life. One can rise in life through flattery. It is a very good investment which brings a good reward. A worker can get quick promotion by flattering his employer. Flattery is food for some bosses and they like to be flattered by their subordinates. Persons in high places have a number of flatterers around them. The more important position a person holds, the larger is the number of flatterers around him. A scholar feels flattered if we praise his scholarship. An athlete feels flattered if we praise his physical prowess. An orator feels flattered if we compliment him on his gift of the gab.

A mother feels flattered if we praise her child. We should be lavish in our praise of others. We should not be half-hearted or luke-warm and must flatter a person enthusiastically and without any reservations.

Women like men to flatter them and the simplest way to flatter women is to tell them that they are very beautiful and intelligent. Even a plain woman likes to be complimented for beauty. If we tell a woman that she is very glamorous, she is sure to like our company. An old woman will feel flattered if we tell her that she is young for her years. Even stern and harsh-looking persons can be won over by flattery.

Even Julius Caesar who claimed to hate flatterers, felt most flattered when he was told that he did not like flattery. Before flattering someone we should make sure that he or she is in the right mood. We should not flatter anybody at the wrong occasion. ●

51. Charity

Charity is one of the noblest virtues of man. A charitable person is a lover of humanity. He has sympathy with his fellow-men and he likes to help others in distress. Charity can be exercised in several ways. A beggar may not get anything from a hard-hearted and callous person. On the contrary, a charitable person would surely give some relief to the beggar at his door. A man of charitable disposition feels moved when he sees victims of natural calamities such as floods, earthquakes, riots etc. and he contributes his mite to relieve people in distress.

It is common knowledge that a charitable person contributes liberally to such relief funds. It is the spirit of charity which prompts people to send woollen clothes, food, money and other material help to the unfortunate brethren who have been the victims of some natural calamity. Charity is a noble sentiment.

However, every human being is not charitable. If this were so, no country in the world would suffer the pangs of hunger and poverty. It is sad that some countries have enough and to spare while inhabitants of other countries live below the poverty line. However, injudicious charity is harmful. The charitable persons should show the spirit of charity only to deserving persons. Indiscriminate charity gives rise to a class of people called parasites.

Also, one should not trumpet one's charity. However, in the present times most charitable persons show charity for publicity or to win social kudos. Such persons are hypocrites. The best form of charity is one when the identity of the donor remains hidden. ●

CHAPTER 3

PARAGRAPHS

Superstitions

Superstitions cut across caste, communal and even national boundaries. People all over the world have superstitions, though they may differ from country to country and region to region. The origin of superstitions can be traced to the element of fear; the urge for security and material welfare. In the western civilisation, one of the most well-known superstitions is the ill-luck which number thirteen is supposed to bring. Also, in the West, passing under a ladder is considered unlucky.

There are many superstitions which are prevalent in India. If a black cat runs across someone's path, it is believed, the person will either meet with an accident or fail in his mission. Hooting of the owl is supposed to bring disaster in the neighbourhood, or to the particular house he is sitting on. Cawing of the crow announces the arrival of some guests. Wailing of a dog foreshadows death. If one meets a Brahmin immediately on setting out for a job, one is most likely to fail. On the other hand, if one meets a sweeper, it is supposed to bring success. Looking at an empty vessel at the time of coming out of the house is also supposed to bring failure. If someone sneezes, when one is getting ready to go out to accomplish a task, he is likely to fail. People don't like to be called back and questioned when they are setting out for some work. Women's braids are hung at the back of vehicles in order to ward off the evil eye. A newly built house has to ward off the evil eye. This is done by hanging on the facade of the house an ugly, fearsome face, usually painted black.

Some of the superstitions are, however, supposed to bring about good luck. Finding of a horse shoe and carrying it along, is considered a sign of good luck. A strange phenomenon about superstitions is that even when in actual life many of them do not come true, people continue to cling to them. Superstitions fill men with anxiety and fear unnecessarily, leading to nervous strain. ●

Competition

Life has become very fast and much complicated in the modern world. There is cut-throat competition everywhere as this is the age of competition. If a person is slow and sluggish, he is automatically thrown out of the competition. Keeping pace with the prevalent time and conditions, it is essential that we are fast and sure so that we can come out with flying colours in any competition. Healthy competition is a good process as it spurs as to outshine and outsmart others. It makes us put all our energies to their best use and sharpens our tools which lead to success. The absence of competition makes us slack and lethargic. Competition compels a businessman work faster so that he can turn the market in his favour. He learns news means to attract customers. He also tries to improve the quality of the products for the benefit of the consumer.

Competition also makes the prices go down so that the demand for goods increases. Those who are slow lag behind and are left out of the game of life. As they can't compete, success eludes them. Average students do not get admission in good schools or colleges and fail to qualify for any competitive examination. They lag behind and their careers remain dark. They fail to get due respect in the society as they have to work in servitude, always at the mercy of others. It is only through competition that the winners are able to push ahead leaving those unfit for competition behind. ●

Fashions

Man has always been a slave of traditions, customs, conventions, ceremonies and rituals. Similarly, human beings are also the slaves of changing fashions. In respect of fashion in dress even people of modest means feel impelled to follow changing fashions. In matters of dress women are much greater slaves to fashions than men. The worst-affected section of this tyranny of modern fashions is our school and college going populace. Fashion in latest made dresses dominates the large majority of them. Almost all students regard fashion as an essential part of their duty to march with the times and thus appear up-to-date and modern. Girls as well as boys spend much of their precious time preening themselves. They are skilled judges in the matter of dress and eye one another's clothes with keen interest. Each tries to excel others in the beauty and design of his clothes. Students who are expensively dressed claim special privileges in the college because they think that their costly clothes are an additional qualification. The same applies to the theatre, dance, music, concerts and 'art' exhibitions. Many people belonging to the upper class go to these places, not because they have any real taste for or understanding of music or art but they want to be 'in the swim'. They would feel backward if they were not to visit these shows and be seen there, and if they were not able to talk about these things afterwards in their respective circles.

The results of this dandyism are terrible. Students pay no attention to class lectures. They look appreciatively at their own nicely-cut suits and are filled with a sort of self-satisfaction. The teachers are helpless in this matter resulting in an increase in the number of fops. Such students, evidently, do not take interest in their studies and going to college is a mere hobby or recreation for them, and examinations and class lectures an evil. Fashions are more prevalent in metropolitan cities where they come into vogue, find ever-increasing favour among the youth and then spread like an 'epidemic'. Movies also cast their maximum influence on the young boys and girls. Craze for pop music, long hair among boys and short-hair among girls are the other spheres of fashions. The moralists feel that modern fashions are an encouragement to crime and should be curbed and stopped but they are helpless. ●

Two Faces of a Big City

Big cities of our country such as Delhi, Mumbai, Chennai and Kolkata have two faces. Millions of people live in a big city. Some people here, are very rich but some are very poor. Also, there is substantial middle-class population. The life of its inhabitants is very hectic as there is cut-throat competition in every field and a mad race for money is always on. The rich people have every thing at their beck and call as they enjoy everything which money can buy. The luxurious life they lead puts to shame the kings and queens of the by-gone days. They earn and spend money like water and are said to be rolling in wealth. They spend their evenings in the most expensive hotels and clubs and enjoy the most expensive foods and wines. They have little time to spend with their families and children. Their adolescent children fall victims to many bad habits in the prime of their youth as they indulge in all sort of activities without any hindrance from any side.

The other face of a big city is the abject poverty. The poor whose troubles are èndless, struggle their whole life to make both ends meet. They get nectar only in a sieve. The poor live in slums, sleep on dusty footpaths and are unable to get even a square meal. Their children are deprived of education, proper clothes, medicine and even potable water. They are made to work right from infancy and have to resort to selling wares and even beg for their survival. Their womenfolk also have to undergo all sorts of sufferings for mere survival. Thus, the poor are born penniless and they die penniless.

The so-called elite class is self-centred and is not ready even to look at or hear about the dwellers of jhuggies and the very existence of the poor is unbearable to them. No one is ready to extend a helping hand to the downtroddens of their society. ●

Habit is Second Nature

Constant use of a thing makes us its prey. For a man who has smoked cigar for two decades, it is as important if not more than the very food. A city dweller who is used to the comforts of an air-conditioner would find himself in hell, if the authority supplying electricity forces him to put it off to save power consumption. There will be virtual chaos in the life of newspaper readers, if the newspaper offices are closed down for one week.

Habits may be good as well as bad. Good habits are an asset whereas bad habits are a curse. Honesty, truth, compassion, kindness are good habits. Having a feeling of compassion for the poor and those who are less privileged is considered a divine habit. These habits make us experience joy and success in all walks of our life. Violence, dishonesty, cruelty are bad habits which lead to our ultimate ruin. Smoking, gambling and drinking may give us temporary pleasure but they ruin us in the long run. Students who are early-risers and attend school in time, go for a walk, respect their teachers, parents and elders and who do not mix up in bad company are an asset to their school, home and society as a whole. Bad habits if repeated many times will stay with us for ever. So it is better we repeat good habits many times which will lead to our well-being, success and prosperity. ●

God Helps Those Who Help Themselves

A hardworking man is bound to achieve success in his life. The proverb 'God helps those who help themselves' is very apt and universally recognised as a beacon for practical life. God certainly helps those who earnestly work and put in their best efforts in whatever field they are in. Those who wait for God's bounty to fall on them always remain disappointed. If we put our heart and soul in our work, success will certainly knock at our door and we shall get further motivation from our colleagues and masters.

The habit of self-help stands us in good stead. A hard working and self-dependent person outshines and becomes an ideal for others. He gets God's blessings, self confidence, respect and goodwill from others and earns a name for himself. One who is sincere, honest, who never thinks of doing an evil to others and whose conscience is clear is loved and helped by God. Such a person faces no impediments in his life and he goes on succeeding at every milestone of life, finally reaching his destination. ●

Dignity of Labour

All must reorganise the dignity of labour and no work should be considered as inferior or lowly. All men do some or the other type of work to keep themselves alive. Some may be very rich businessmen or highly placed officials in the government or private sector. Others have to labour hard to keep themselves alive. Some have to dig, drive and till the soil or work at a mill and do many other things to keep the body and soul together. They may find their work hard, unpleasant but there is no escape from it as life and labour are inseparable.

The indignity attached to manual work is the outcome of division of labour. Unlike the simple and less complex society of the olden days when the high and the low did normal work, the complex nature of modern society and the introduction of machinery have been responsible to a great extent for perpetuating this sense of indignity. This distinction arises when some jobs are left only for the common man while some are kept reserved for the privileged. Some people grow to be powerful, rich and important and finding the manual work too hard for them, keep it for the common man.

In fact, the work done by the so-called common man is more important. The labourer, the peasant, the sweeper and the mill worker and factory worker are responsible for giving us food, houses and all other necessities and luxuries which man, rich or poor, needs. The work done by this class of society should never be considered as mean or inferior. One will not derive happiness if he is reminded that the work he is doing is inferior and mean. Men who are engaged in manual labour must be made to feel the worth of their work. On manual labour depends the life of the world and hence is the aptness of the proverb "work is worship". ●

Man does not Live by Bread Alone

Like other animals man needs food for his survival and subsistence. The needs of all men biologically or physiologically are like those of other animals. Man may get his food or he may earn it. Sometimes he has to resort to grabbing it, procuring it or stealing it. He has to run around till he satiates this basic necessity. However, while the other animals after getting food rest contented, man looks around to fulfil his mental, intellectual and spiritual needs.

All the works of art, literature, science, philosophy speak amply of man's insatiable hunger for making progress and taking strides ahead in the direction of progress, prosperity and development. Had man confined his goal in life to only fulfilling his physical appetite, no nations could have progressed and there would have been complete stagnation. There is no doubt that life poses innumerable problems to man but it also offers many challenges. Man has accepted the challenges happily and has crossed what once seemed to be unsurmountable impediments. ●

Politics is the Art of Compromise

Every game has its own rules and regulations. Also, it has some ethics and principles and all the participants in the game are expected to abide by the code and conduct of the game and to adhere to certain norms. Politics, however, is an exception. It has absolutely no rules, no track, no clear-cut or defined path, no set principles and no ethical code.

It is an art of compromise and adjustment. In politics, one sees the situation, position and watches the direction of the wind and then takes action. One cannot afford the unyielding, unbending and uncompromising nature of Satan.

Like Eliot's concept of a mature poet, man has to continually surrender his personality and individuality. He has to become the mouth-piece or mouth organ of the public. He has to constantly watch the public mood and take further steps accordingly. Thus, a successful politician is a watchman of people's mind and moods. However, there is no doubt that there have been politicians who have influenced, changed and guided the masses and have left a permanent impact on people's mind. ●

Must We Learn English ?

English, being a foreign language and having a British origin, does not belong to India. But it has developed into an international language and the time has come when we cannot do without this language. It seems that English has come to stay. The developments made in science and technology, the great art and literature of the world and international media are available in the English language. We can not afford to be ignorant of all these things. All other regional languages of the world cannot compete with English.

India, being an underdeveloped country, cannot afford to ignore the world of media thereby lagging behind in the fast developing society of the world. India must keep abreast with all the developments of the world and make the present and next generations knowledgeable citizens of the world.

There should be no prejudice about learning English, as English has become the only link language among all countries of the world. We can not afford translations as a huge sum is incurred in this process. Having good command over spoken and written English enables our youth to get jobs in the international job market. As the world is developing into a single entity, it matters least to which country one belongs. Being well-versed in this language is the minimum eligibility today, to try for the lucrative jobs. ●

Social Service

It is rightly said that service done to mankind is service done to God. Man, being a social animal lives in a society. God has created man so that he can help the needy and serve those who are handicapped, less privileged and downtrodden. We must not look to our welfare only but to the people around us who are leading woesome lives. Doomed are those who are jealous of others and who want only themselves to be healthy, happy, rich and prosperous. One can be happy only if one grows along with others.

Gone are the days when there was only one rich man in a village who enjoyed all the luxuries of life and the others around him bowed to him for all sorts of help and lived in his servitude. They came into this world to lick the soles of the only rich man and died obeying and serving him. Now there has been a tremendous change and no one can exploit the rights of others.

So in the new society we must change our attitude and work for the welfare of our fellow human beings and even lower animals, especially the poor and the neglected. We must know who around us need our help and who are depressed and illiterate. Those who are sick and poor, who can not make both ends meet, who cannot give vent to their feelings and sorrows, must get our help. Some people are compelled to turn to crime because of extreme poverty. Some are paid very low wages and some only pittance. We must become their benefactors.

Mother Teresa set an example which is unparalleled in human history. She provided a home to the shelterless, gave her love and compassion to those who needed them most. She crossed all barriers of caste, creed, nation, religion, sex and boundaries. She embraced the poor and the sick and healed the wounds of their minds and hearts. She looked after the lepers and provided solace and peace to their gloomy hearts. ●

An Ideal Citizen

An ideal citizen is an institution in itself. He is an asset to the family, society around him and the country as a whole. He has a certain standard of life in everything. He loves his country, countrymen and is a great well-wisher of all mankind. He does not discriminate any one on the basis of caste, colour, creed, religion or riches. He is a friend to all and foe to none.

An ideal citizen is a true patriot who loves people of all nations, religions and sects equally. He abides by the laws of the land and protests strongly if any one breaks the law. He despises socials evils such as corruption, caste distinctions, exploitation of women, children and the poor strata of society.

He is tolerant in all matters and does not turn violent or rebellious. He possesses the highest moral character and is selfless in all matters. He believes in the dignity of labour and work is worship to him. He revolts against hoarding, thieving, cheating, smuggling and black-marketing. He is not a silent spectator and revolts against all social evils. He has a great moral courage and is ever ready to face trouble as a consequence of his protests. He tolerates patiently. The sincerity of his thoughts, actions and will provides him extra courage to fight these evils. He defies the offers of corrupt officers, black marketers, smugglers and hoarders and exposes them in public. He is a real asset who is loved by the Almighty. ●

Righteousness Exalteth a Nation

Righteousness always plays an important role in life. It may be the life of an individual, a family, a state or a nation. No doubt, money, power and pelf can provide the comforts and luxuries of life but all these can not provide mental satisfaction and spiritual contentment. The religious and spiritual leaders have always advised mankind to shun the path of vice, glamour, glitter and luxury and follow the path of righteousness. Such leaders have done so in the past, are doing so in the present and will continue to advise the future generations.

A nation can exalt itself only when it cares for its poor, nurses its old and feeble, looks after its downtrodden and weaker sections of society and checks exploitation. All great nations are built on the morals of their citizens. The moment the citizens of any nation become unscrupulous, the nation collapses. Nations have risen to meteoric heights when they follow the right path. Righteousness truly exalteth a nation because it takes a nation far on the road to progress. ●

He who Conquers Himself is Mighty

There is no doubt that almost every person can preach and win over a few admirers by his oration, by the use of a few high sounding words and with the proclamation of his ideals. However, the problem arises when the person himself has to abide by these preachings. Alexander conquered quite a few parts of the world but failed to exercise control over his own self.

It was Gautama, the Buddha who conquered his desires, yearnings and passions. The world, unfortunately, has known many ruthless tyrants like Nadir Shah who conquered, killed and enslaved others. But their victories could not last. No man on the earth held them in esteem. On the other hand, the name of Ashoka shines in the history of the world. He is remembered not because he won the great battle of Kalinga but because he left no stone unturned in serving humanity and exercised restraint over his own self. What counts is the strength of the mind and not the might of the muscles. ●

Brevity is the Soul of Wit

Most people all over the world have no patience and time for repetition and circumlocution. They look for crisp and pithy sayings. Short stories and one-act plays have been greatly admired and accepted by the people but the thousand page romances have been shunned by most. Bacon and Pope are still enjoyed the world over while Spencer and Milton are read only by the scholars. Brevity brings out exactness, aptness and appropriateness. Long winding speeches often tax the public nerve and create monotony. A few well-chosen words prove more effective than rhetorical speeches. What is most desired by the people is more matter with less art. Unusually long sentences can not draw and retain one's attention, while on the other hand we are enchanted by short, pithy and effective sentences. Compression of thought wins public applause as it is an art. ●

Sweet are the Uses of Adversity

When a man is prosperous, he is surrounded by fair-weather friends. But during adversity such friends disappear. Good times make a man complacent, lazy and lethargic. However adverse times bring the best in man and awaken him. He becomes alert, agile and starts kicking. When fortune smiles on man, he forgets himself and even becomes oblivious of the existence of God. He embraces pride, vanity and hautiness and moves out for sensual pleasures. Man realises his follies and blunders only when bad luck strikes him again and again. Then he tries to repent, lament, chasten and purify himself. He wants to make up for his past blunders. Then only he understands the real meaning and purpose of life. Emerson has said, "Poverty is the most perfect of all institutions". John Milton called poverty the "eternal companion of the wisest". Those who fought the toughest battles of life won the highest laurels. ●

We Live in Deeds and Not in Years

On an odd occasion, we do find a very old man making news for no other reason, but for a very long though unfruitful life. But he would not be remembered the way Keats and Shalley are remembered in the history of English literature or the young sons of Guru Gobind Singh who were bricked alive for the steadfastness of their religion and faith. People are remembered for their selfless service to humanity. The names of Mahatma Gandhi, Sardar Patel, Netaji Subhash Chandra Bose and Sardar Bhagat Singh, Raj Guru and Sukh Dev have been inscribed in the history of independence struggle of our country because of their valour, dedication, nobility, steadfastness, courage and conviction. Life is not merely breathing and dwelling but thought and action. Life is a challenge worth accepting. Heroic deeds do not necessarily need a long life for their performance. Alexander did not take many years to conquer a sizable portion of the known world. ●

Neither a Borrower Nor a Lender Be

Money is the root of all troubles and is at the back of almost all the crimes and murders the world over. Leave apart the external struggle which more or less, all of us undergo to pocket it, there is an internal strife in the family itself which throws apart father and son, brother and brother, husband and wife, sister and brother at an unbridgeable distance. Members of many families face each other in civil and criminal courts of the country. It speaks volumes of the role played and havoc created by money. The cases of friends losing their life-long friendship because of the involvement of money and becoming arch-enemies are not unknown. Hence it is better to spend only what you earn and save a little so that you have not to look to any one for financial help. It is a golden rule. However a question can be posed, "What else are friends for in case they have to draw back their hand at the hour of the need ? ●

All That Glitters is not Gold

Wearing of a gown would not make an idiot a professor, nor would he be able to pass off like a lawyer. His foolishness would still be revealed by his face. Painting and powdering the face may attract the attention of a passerby but it would not take him long to find out the truth. A layman, on finding a shining base metal, may imagine it to be gold, but the goldsmith would soon reveal the truth to him which will be to his dismay. However, there are many fakes and quacks who successfully play the roles of qualified people. Fake and standard things, sell fairly well, because of the false propaganda and advertisement about them. Many youngsters run to Bollywood attracted by the false glitter and glamour of the film industry. ●

Where There is a Will there is Way

Some persons such as Napoleon, Shivaji, Gandhiji, Lincoln and others have proved to the world that whatever the odds, the impediments, the obstacles, the hurdles, one can attain anything and everything in the world if one has will, determination, courage, endurance and perseverance. Physical infirmities, bodily diseases, mental anguish can never prevent a spirited and determined soldier from fighting his way in life. Opposition of a sizable section of America could not deter Lincoln in his plan of abolishing slavery from the United States of America. The massacre of innocent persons at Jalianwala Bagh in Amritsar did not instill fear in the hearts of patriotic Indians from going ahead with their plans of liberating the country from the yoke of the British rule. However, sometimes, chance and fate conspire against man and upset his plans. ●

The Pen is Mightier than the Sword

The sword in the present time plays a subordinate role to the pen. It is moved, directed, ordered and commanded by the pen. An order of the American President can make thousands of armed men to take action and destroy the vast empire. The maker, the framer, the creator of the atomic bomb formula is certainly more powerful than a swordsman who can boast of beating many at a time at his game. The days of the glory of men with muscles have passed. A writer can instigate a whole nation to revolt as he can play upon the sentiments and emotions of the people. He can also play the part of a peace-maker, an assuager, who can pacify the emotionally surcharged people. No one can doubt the role of the Press in the present time and Shakespeare is certainly valued more today than Changez Khan. ●

Knowledge is Power

While the word 'power' has all along been associated with muscular strength, the word 'knowledge' is connected with the mind. The two words do not seem to have any connection whatsoever. However, today the word power has undergone a tremendous transformation. To day it is recognised that the pen is mightier than the sword. A brainy person and not a muscular person is considered important and a more useful citizen of the society. The present society respects psychologists, philosophers and literary men who make great contributions for mankind. A scientist, though physically weak or even wreck can cause a destruction which hundreds of able-bodied men cannot even dream of. Whatever comfort and luxuries we enjoy today are the direct result of the study and inventions of men of knowledge. ●

Honesty is the Best Policy

As the world has seen people enjoying the fruits of their ill-gotten wealth and leading luxurious lives indulging in all sorts of sensual pleasures, the proverb — Honesty is the Best Policy — has often been laughed at. However, we probably forget to see the difference in the inner and outer personality of such people. We watch and feel thrilled by their glamour and glasses of whisky. But what goes underneath their glasses of whisky and how fast their hearts beat remain unascertained. Such persons can never have peace of mind and contentment. Their eyes are always vigilant as if they are detecting something or fearing being detected. 'Ends justify means', is the saying of those persons who live in the world of illusions. Means ultimately matter and play an important role. If Mahatma Gandhi is remembered and worshipped today, it is because none would ever dare question his honesty, sincerity, nobility and the means, the mode, the methods employed by him. A person's esteem in the eyes of the world can be raised only by honesty. Dishonest persons may enjoy the fruits but they are transitory and it is only honesty which brings lasting benefits and also complete peace of mind. ●

Liberty cannot Exist without Discipline

Liberty can only be maintained permanently if we subject ourselves to rules, regulations and discipline. The case of a woman in England who wanted to walk in the middle of a busy road, as her country had got independence, is well-known. She did not understand the meaning of liberty precisely and thought it an implied licence to do whatever one liked. In fact, discipline is necessary and a must for every branch of life, may it be a lecture in a classroom, or political meeting or travelling in a bus. If one oversteps one's rights, one becomes responsible for curtailing others' rights. Besides, one ought to know that rights imply duties and without duties rights would be meaningless. We are sure to create disorder and chaos for ourselves and for our country if we do not honour discipline. Discipline alone can keep these menaces away and prevent the law of jungle from prevailing. ●

Make Hay While the Sun Shines

Opportunities make their appearances once in a while and vanish before long. They do not come for the mere asking. Those who are alert, agile, smart and on the lookout for opportunities, catch and put them to best use, while the lazy, lethargic, inactive and weak wait for them to come and share bed with them. The secret of all the successful men the world over is that they do not lazily wait and watch but act, move and grab opportunities. One should not keep on crying over spilt milk, as this is futile. and one should do one's best leaving no stone unturned while the time is favouring us. We should know to play our cards carefully else we may have to repent and suffer irreparable loss. We must be very watchful of the sun when it shines and then make hay. ●

Fools Rush in Where Angels Fear to Tread

An intelligent person would first like to evaluate the chances of his success and would take the required precautions before taking a plunge. However a fool would be too easily lured by the glitter and would be ever ready to make a leap in the dark. Fools lack reasoning, understanding, commonsense and power to comprehend. Any person devoid of these traits is not aware whether he is treading the purgatory or the heaven. Poloniuses the world over jump to conclusions without substantiating the evidences and it is only Hamlets who strongly desire to probe deep, be sure and only then resort to action. However the world is full of Rosencrantzs and Guildensterns who find themselves capable of probing and knowing the mysteries of the hearts of the people. ●

CHAPTER 4

FORMAL LETTERS

Write a letter to the Manager Sales ONIDA, New Delhi complaining about the defects in the T.V. set purchased by you and also request for its replacement.

B-92 SFS Flats
Hari Nagar
New Delhi-110036

February 9, 20...

The Manager Sales
ONIDA, Janakpuri
New Delhi-110036

Subject : Defective T.V. Set

Sir

I regret to inform you that I purchased a colour T.V. Model E84 from your Janakpuri showroom vide Bill No. 3284, dated January 28, 20....

However, the T.V. started giving trouble immediately after its purchase. An engineer came to rectify the set twice, after I made a complaint. But the same trouble is still persisting. The picture is not clear and the sound is accompanied with some unwanted noise.

I therefore request you to kindly replace this T.V. set as per the rules of your company.

Thanking you

Yours sincerely

Rakesh

Write a letter to the General Manager, MTNL (South Delhi 1) complaining against your phone which has been dead for the last 20 days, inspite of repeated complaints.

Flat No. 79
AC-Block, Haus Khas
New Delhi-110016

January 16, 20...

Subject : Dead Telephone

Sir

I regret to bring to your kind notice that my telephone No. 26518408 installed at the above stated address has been dead for more than 20 days.

The complaint was booked on 198 on 26 December 20... and the complaint No. was 238. On 3rd January, 20... I was given a fresh complaint No. 118 but the telephone is till dead.

I am facing great inconvenience due to this erratic telephone which has not been rectified even after a lapse of 20 days.

I therefore request you to kindly direct the concerned staff members to rectify my telephone immediately.

Thanking you

Yours faithfully

K.K. Lall

Write a letter to the SHO of your area inviting his attention to the growing incidents of thefts in your area.

The SHO
Police Station
Haus Khas
New Delhi-110016

Subject : Growing incidents of thefts

Sir

I would like to draw your kind attention to the frequent incidents of thefts in Haus Khas. Ten cases of thefts were reported during the last 15 days.

Besides thefts, a car was stolen yesterday from J-block of Haus Khas. It seems that there is an organised gang which is responsible for this. Not a single case of theft has been solved and neither any arrests been made to far. The beat constables and residential guards have no clue as to who is responsible for these thefts. The residents are angry and scared.

Keeping the above in view, you are requested to initiate a special drive to nab the culprits and bring them to book so that the confidence of the residents is restored.

Thanking you

Yours faithfully

K.C. Nath

Write a letter to the Principal requesting him to issue you the School Leaving Certificate, as your father has been transferred outside Delhi. You are Rakesh Ahuja of IX class.

The Principal
Laxman Public School
Haus Khas Enclave
New Delhi-110016

September 18, 20...

Subject : School Leaving Certificate

Sir

Most humbly and respectfully I beg to state that my father has been transferred to Jaipur and we are all leaving with him for Jaipur.

Although it was my strong desire to complete my Board examination while studying in the prestigious Laxman

Public School, I am compelled to leave this school due to unavoidable circumstances.

I therefore request you to kindly issue me School Leaving Certificate.

Thanking you

Yours obediently

Rakesh Ahuja

IX–D

You are Dibyansh of C-10, Kalkaji Extension, New Delhi-110039. Write a letter of complaint to the Police Commissioner of your city telling him that the nuisance of loudspeakers continues in your neighbourhood in spite of the fact that its use has been banned by the authorities.

C-10
Kalkaji Extension
New Delhi-110039

July 23, 20...

The Police Commissioner
Police Headquarters
New Delhi

Subject : Nuisance of Loudspeakers

Sir

I regret to draw your kind attention to the incessant blaring of loud speakers in our area.

Places of worship of all the religions vie with one another in preaching their messages, each louder than the other. Loudspeakers blare from the roof tops of more or less all these places. The volume of these loudspeakers causes great inconvenience not only to students, especially when they are preparing for their examinations but also to the old and infirm people who are deprived of peace and harmony.

The residents of our area have appealed on many occasions to the managers of these religious places but all our requests have fallen on deaf ears and this nuisance continues unabated in spite of the fact that their use has been legally banned.

Keeping the above in view, I request you on behalf of the residents, to depute an officer who can look into the matter and initiate suitable action.

Thanking you

Yours faithfully

Dibyansh

You have a degree in Marketing Management and have worked for a firm for about seven years. Write an application for a job to XYZ Consultants, Okhla Phase-II, New Delhi, in response to their advertisement in the Hindustan Times. You are Vivek of ABC Colony, Ghaziabad.

ABC Colony
Ghaziabad, U.P.

June 6, 20...

Personnel Manager
XYZ Consultants
Okhla Phase II
New Delhi

Subject : Application for the Post of Senior Marketing Manager

Sir

This has reference to your advertisement in the Hindustan Times dated, Ist June for the post of Senior Marketing Manager and I offer my services as one of the candidates.

My work experience, educational qualification and other particulars are mentioned in my resume, enclosed at the end of the letter. Names and addresses of two persons as my references have also been included. In fact, I am looking for a challenging position where I can put my potential to the best use.

I assure you that if I am found suitable for the post, I'll put my best efforts to discharge my duties diligently and with integrity.

Thanking you

Yours faithfully

Vivek

Enclosures : (1) Resume

(2) Copies of testimonials

(3) Experience certificate from the previous employer

RESUME

Name	:	
Father's name	:	
Date of birth	:	
Complete address	:	
Educational qualification	:	
Work experience	:	
Hobbies and interests	:	
Languages known	:	
Any special achievement	:	
Reference	:	

Write a letter to the Health Officer of your locality complaining against the deplorable condition of the roads, streets of your area.

B-48, Hari Nagar
New Delhi-110063

3rd October 20...

The Health Officer
Hari Nagar Area
New Delhi

Subject : Deplorable Conditions

Sir

I would like to draw your kind attention to the deplorable condition of lanes, streets and roads of Hari Nagar B-block area.

There are heaps of garbage on the streets and roads. The garbage has not been removed for months. The drains are also chocked and the water overflows on the roads and lanes. There is a stink all over the place and there are big holes and ditches in many areas. A few complaints were lodged with the concerned authorities but in vain. Only once, the municipality lorry removed the garbage of one area and the existing state of affairs has further worsened as many children have been affected by this squalor. Some children are suffering from cholera and malaria. The whole area has become a breeding place for mosquitoes and there is danger of an epidemic breaking out.

You are kindly requested to take personal interest to get this area cleaned of the stinking garbage and improve other sanitary conditions.

Thanking you

Yours faithfully

Harkesh

For Residents of Hari Nagar

Write a letter to the Postmaster, Post Office Malviya Nagar, drawing his attention to the non-receipt of a money-order you sent to your father in Punjab.

A-1 Shivalik Apartments
Malviya Nagar
New Delhi-110017
June 3rd, 20...

The Post Master
Post Office, Malviya Nagar
New Delhi-110017

Subject : Non-delivery of Money Order

Sir

I booked a money order for Rupees five hundred addressed to my father Mr. Adesh, Gali No. 3, New Colony Batala on 5th May 20.... The money order was booked from your Sub Post Office, Pushp Vihar, Sector V. vide receipt No. 0328, dated, 5th May 20....

The money order has not yet been delivered to the addressee even after the lapse of about one month. This is a matter of grave concern and a real shock. My father has been greatly inconvenienced due to the non-receipt of the money. You are therefore requested to kindly initiate prompt action to trace out the missing money-order.

Thanking you
Yours faithfully
Ajay Sood

Write a letter to Academic Publishers, New Delhi complaining against the parcel of books which you received only yesterday.

Flat No. 28
MIG Old Scheme Saket
New Delhi-110-017

May 7, 20...

Academic Publishers
28/3 Nai Sarak
Delhi-110005

Subject : Defective Books

Sir

This has reference to my order for eight books dated 25th April, 20.... I regret to bring to your notice that I received the packet of books yesterday but two books — English Grammar with Answers by Dr. Jaina and Unique Comprehension by Madan Sood — were not found in the parcel and the book — Useful Idioms and Phrases — is defective. It has a few pages missing and a few torn. I am sending this book back to you.

The receipt of defective books and non-receipt of two books have put me to great inconvenience. All the eight books have been billed by you and I have already paid the money as the books were sent through V.P.P.

You are therefore requested to send me the missing books and replace the enclosed defective book immediately.

Thanking you

Yours faithfully

Anand Kohli

You are the captain of your school cricket team. Write a letter to the Principal of your school requesting his permission to play a friendly cricket match with the local cricket club.

Boys Hostel
M.N.R.V. School
Dwarka
New Delhi

4th March, 20...

The Principal
M.N.R.V. School
Dwarka, New Delhi

Sir

Most humbly and respectfully, I would like to bring to your kind notice that I have received an offer from the captain of the local cricket club Sahara Eleven, to play a friendly cricket match with our school cricket team in the play ground of our school.

I therefore request you on behalf of our school cricket team to kindly grant formal permission for the match to be played in our school play ground, as and when it is convenient to you. The permission may be granted after consultation with the school sports incharge.

It will be a good opportunity for our school cricket team to play a match with an outside team.

Thanking you

Yours obediently

Karan

Captain
School Cricket Team

CHAPTER 5

INFORMAL LETTERS

Write a letter to your friend who lives in a far-off village in Himachal Pradesh requesting him to spend some days with you in Delhi.

D-84, Kusumbhi Apartments
Greater Kailash
New Delhi-110048

January 3rd, 20...

Dear Sohail

I got your letter yesterday and was happy to know that you are going to have a few days' holiday.

I wish that you should come to Delhi for one week. Here we shall visit all the historical places such as the Red Fort, Qutub Minar, Humayun Tomb, India Gate, Purana Quila. There are many other places which are worth-seeing such as museums, parks, zoo, Appu Ghar, etc.

Although you may not like Delhi for its air pollution, noise pollution and the mad rush of people, yet it would certainly provide a great change which one enjoys on visiting any new place. Besides, Delhi like any other metropolitan city has its own beauty which is good for the soul and body. Please do come along with your parents and younger sister, if possible.

Hope to see you soon.

Your loving friend
Akash

You are Ankit. Write a letter to your father who has expressed his displeasure on your bad performance in your examination, assuring him of better performance in your forthcoming examination.

A-48,
Vasundhra Enclave
Ghaziabad, U.P.

1st January 20...

My dear Father

I got your letter yesterday and I am really very sorry to have disappointed you by faring badly in my examination.

I admit that I did not do well in the examination as I had neglected my studies and the result is obvious.

I once again express my regret to have disappointed you. However, I have resolved to study seriously for the coming examinations which are due next month. I will not let you down and work hard to compensate for the loss.

I hope that you will forgive me for my negligence and bless me to do well in future. Also, kindly assure mother that I have determined to channelise all my energy in studies.

I once again apologise for my negligence.

Pay my regards to mother.

Your loving son
Ankit

Write a letter to your friend who has failed in the Board examination, motivating him not to lose heart and work hard for the next time.

C-48
Lajpat Nagar II
New Delhi-110038

February 8, 20...

Dear Rahul

It was really disheartening to know that you have not been able to succeed in your Board examination. I know that you really worked hard and did not deserve to fail.

Your failure may be attributed to your being bed-ridden for some days before the examination.

As failure is also part of life it should be accepted and there is nothing to lose heart. What cannot be cured must be endured. All great persons have experienced failures in their lives.

You should now come out of this and put renewed efforts to prepare for the Board examination due next year. I hope that you will succeed with flying colours next time.

Pay my regards to your parents.

Your loving friend

Rakesh

You are Chirag. Write a letter of Condolence to your friend who has lost his father in an accident.

C-35, Ordnance Society
Dwarka Sector 13
New Delhi

5th January, 20...

Dear Abhishek

I was shocked to hear the untimely demise of your beloved father in a road accident. There is no doubt that it is a bolt from the blue and there can't be anything more distressing. Strange are the ways of God and all human beings are insignificant creatures in front of the Almighty who decides our destinies. There is no cure for this tragedy except to submit before the will of God. You will have to bear with this great loss and reconcile yourself with this irreparable loss.

What cannot be cured must be endured. In the current crisis you have to be bold and face this situation with great courage. Only fortitude and a strong will, will enable you to face this misfortune.

May God rest the departed soul in peace and give you and all dears and nears courage enough to face this loss boldly.

Yours sincerely

Chirag

Your are Sonali studying in Father Agnel School, Dehra Doon. You have received a letter from your father who has asked you to describe your new school. Write this letter to your father.

Father Agnel School

Dehra Doon

26th June, 20...

My dear Father

I received your letter last week but I am sorry I could not write to you immediately about my new school.

I am quite hale and hearty and happy in the new school. This school is quite different from the one I last attended.

The girls are quite nice and the teachers are very kind and cooperative. However, I miss my old schoolmates a great deal. I remain busy in my studies during and after the school hours. I take keen interest in English grammar, history, music, dancing and painting. I find maths very dull because, I think, I am not able to grasp the basics of this subject. I hope that I shall pick up soon and start taking interest in maths also.

Also, I have painted a picture which has been appreciated by all. I shall show you this painting when I come home. Rest all is fine over here. We play different games in the play ground of our school.

I am looking forward to meeting you all when the Christmas holidays begin. Give my love to mama and others at home.

Your affectionate daughter,

Sonali

You are Rahul. Your younger brother Rohan is studying in a Boarding school. Write him a letter with a piece of advice to be careful about his studies.

248, Netaji Nagar

New Delhi

June 3, 20...

Dear Rohan

We received your progress report only yesterday and I am pained at your poor performance. I am not able to make out the precise cause of your dismal show. It is just the beginning of your academic year and you seem to have neglected your studies. Try to find out your weak points in all the subjects and gradually devote your time in improving your performance. Do not get disheartened. Devote more time to your studies and work whole-heartedly. You can utilise your time properly by getting up early when the mind is fresh and there is no disturbance.

Practise all the topics carefully and also consult your teachers and friends who are good at studies. Do not shirk work. Also avoid the company of those boys who are not interested in studies as such students bring a bad name to their friends, parents and school.

Nothing is impossible if you make a firm determination and pursue your studies regularly and carefully.

I hope that you will certainly show better performance in your next examination.

Your loving brother

Rahul

You are Kalpana. Yesterday was your birthday and you received a gift from your uncle from abroad. Write a letter of thanks to your uncle.

C-1348, Phase I
New Okhla,
Delhi-42
January 5, 20...

My dear Uncle

Thank you very much for the precious gift you sent me on my birthday which I celebrated yesterday with my friends and parents, with great fun. Yours was the first gift which I received yesterday morning. The man handed a parcel to me wrapped beautifully with a pink ribbon. When I opened the packet, my joy knew no bounds. I was overjoyed to receive the Digital Diary and the beautiful wrist watch with a gold chain.

Every one presented me something and there was a pile of gifts on my birthday which, in fact, was a party with all my friends and my parents. However, the gift sent by you was the best. I missed you greatly on my birthday. Pay my regards to dear aunt and love to Chinkoo.

Your loving niece
Kalpana

You are Ankur. Write a letter to your father from the Boarding school which you joined recently, telling him that you dislike the life of a boarder.

Belham Boys' Hostel
Mussoorie
3rd October 20...

My dear Father

I was very happy to receive your letter yesterday. After reading your letter, I started feeling home-sick. Though I left home only two months ago, it seems decades to me.

In fact, it was much better when I was studying in the day-school and would come home every day. Here I have to stay with another fifteen boys in a big dormitory. Some of these boys are good but many of them, especially the senior ones are always playing nasty jokes on the younger ones. We, being juniors, can not retaliate or they will beat us. Otherwise also, we are bullied by the senior boys most of the time.

These senior boys make us do some or the other work all day.

Please consult mother also and arrange immediately to put me in a day school again.

Your loving son

Ankur

Write a reply to the above letter.

C-16
Greater Kailash-I
New Delhi-110048

8th October, 20...

My dear Ankur

I read your letter and was sad to know that you are not happy in your boarding school. As you have been away from home for the first time, it is natural for you to feel home-sick.

In fact, my dear child, life is not what we want it to be. If I were selfish, I would not allow you to part from your parents and other members. It is very important for all of us to be independent and the sooner it is done, the better. Getting education and growing up to be a complete person is important for all of us so that we can learn to manage our own affairs and stand on our own feet. Your mother is also of the view that all boys should spend a few years at a boarding school.

You must be brave, my dear boy to stick to your school and with the passage of time you will be able to adapt yourself to the new surrounding. Don't mind the jokes the seniors boys play on you. When they come to know that you don't mind their jokes, they will get tired of teasing you.

So cheer up and don't get disheartened.

We look forward to meeting you soon during Christmas holidays.

Your loving Father

....

Write a letter to your friend who has passed the Board examination with high merit, congratulating him on his brilliant success.

Plot No. 128
Pocket 38, Sector-II
Rohini
New Delhi-110058

26th May 20...

Dear Gaurav

Accept my heartiest congratulations on passing the Board examination with flying colours. It is really great news to all of us. My parents are very happy to know about your great success.

In fact, it was expected as you had really worked hard, with sincerity and devotion. Please convey my congratulations to your parents who had very high hopes on you.

What are you planning to do now ? Please let me know. I may suggest that if you join a regular college and complete your graduation in any stream, it will make you eligible to appear for the civil services examination. I know you will certainly make it to the IAS. Even going in for MBA is also a good proposition.

Convey my regards to uncle and aunt and love to Preeti. I hope to hear from you soon.

Yours sincerely

Kailash

You are Sohail. Write a letter to your younger brother who is studying in the Boarding school advising him not to be a complete book-worm and take interest in sports and games also.

C-32
Kailash Hills
New Delhi-110038

September 13, 20...

Dear Akhtar

It is really heartening to know that you have stood first in the class. Your report card also mentions that you are in the very good books of the teachers.

When you came home last time, we all found that you have become weak considerably. I am sure that you are over-exerting yourself in studies and have forgotten completely about sports and games. It is rightly said "All work and no play makes Jack a dull boy".

Academic performance, no doubt, is a prerequisite of student life and nothing can be achieved in life without studies. But there is a strong mind in a strong body. Boys of your age should be bubbling with vigour and vitality. Therefore take care of your physical health also and don't be a book-worm only. Take regular exercise and spare some time for sports and games. Also go for a walk daily in the morning. Remember that only a healthy person can enjoy fully the other achievements of life.

With Love

Your loving brother

Sohail

Last week you had a quarrel with your friend over a trifle. Now you repent and want to apologise. Write a letter to your friend asking an apology for your misbehaviour.

A-248
Subroto Park
New Delhi-110010
July 10, 20...
My dear Ablok
I apologise for the misbehaviour shown to you last week. I don't know why I quarrelled with you without any rhyme or reason. May be I was nursing some anger against something in my mind. I fully realise that it was my fault. I am sorry for by behaviour and therefore I sincerely beg for your forgiveness.
I hope that being older to me, you will forgive me and will not carry any ill-will or bitterness about me. I can't afford to lose a friend as nice as you.
I hope that you will be large-hearted and forgive and forget.
Yours sincerely
Rahul

You recovered after a long illness. Write a letter to your friend stating the present state of your health.

8, Sagar Apartments
Bahadur Shah Marg
New Delhi-110001

29 October, 20...

My dear Rohan

It was really heartening to receive your letter inquiring about my present state of health. I thank you very much for your sympathy for me.

You will be glad to know that after a long bout of illness, I have almost recovered fully. Only some weakness still persists which is natural after a prolonged illness. I have started taking walks and have resumed my studies. I resumed my classes last week. I do feel weak at times but will be alright with the passage of time.

It has all been possible with the help of my doctor and my parents who took very good care of me and of course, the Almighty without whose wish nothing can happen.

I am looking forward to meeting you soon.

Your loving friend
Sohan

You are Rashesh. You want to engage a tutor for Maths and Science. Write a letter to your father seeking his permission to avail the services of a tutor.

AB/N-32
Janakpuri
New Delhi

December 9, 20...

Respected Father

My annual examinations are approaching fast and as you know, I have just recovered from a few days of illness. As I could not attend my classes for about two weeks, I am lagging behind in two subjects Maths and Science.

I, therefore want to engage a tutor who can help me make up the loss in Maths and Science and also clear my doubts. I know that it will be an extra burden on your pocket but I am helpless, as hardly any time is left for the board examinations.

I assure you that I will make the best use of the services of an eminent tutor. Therefore kindly arrange to send the money for the tuition as soon as possible.

Your loving son
Rashesh

Write a letter to your friend living in Shimla sharing with him the problems you have to face in Delhi due to extreme heat and pollution.

B-98, Sukhda Residents Colony
New Delhi-110064

May 2, 20...

Dear Saurabh

I received your letter only yesterday and read the contents. It was really very heartening to read that Shimla has a normal temperature even in the month of May. Temperature in Delhi goes above 43° and there is extreme shortage of water and electricity. Besides, the ever-growing pollution of Delhi adds fuel to the fire.

Shimla is really a heaven on the earth and you are fortunate to be living in Shimla. In Delhi, it is impossible to go out during the afternoon and even in the evening, unless the sun sets and there is some relief in the surroundings. The office-goers are the worst sufferers as they have to sweat it out the whole day. Besides, there is acute shortage of water and electricity due to the increased demand.

The prices of essential commodities also go sky high in the extreme summer here. However, inspite of all these problems, the Delhiites brave it boldly and life is buzzing with activity here.

Your loving friend
Suresh

You have moved to a new house purchased recently. Being very happy, you want to share your happiness with your friend. Write a letter to your friend describing your new house.

98, Kailash Hills
New Delhi-110048

September 12, 20...

My dear Ajay

You will be glad to know that we have purchased a new house. This house is in a posh colony of South Delhi known as Kailash Hills. It is, in fact far-removed from the noise and hum drum of Delhi. This place is full of serenity and calmness, away from din and noise.

Here, we have enough parking place as the adjoining roads are wide and spacious. Our house is a corner plot and open on three sides. It is a duplex house and there are four bed-rooms, drawing-dining and a big living room. There is marble floorings in the whole house. It has a spacious and beautiful kitchen.

The house is airy and well-ventilated. The parking place is also very spacious to accommodate at least three cars. Our neighbours are all educated persons whose company is a great pleasure. I hope that you will visit our new house with your parents soon.

Yours sincerely

Nandan

CHAPTER 6
LETTERS TO EDITOR

You recently read a report that river Yamuna has become a very polluted river. Write a letter to the Editor of the Hindustan Times, expressing your concern. You are Rahul of ABC Colony, Sahadra, Delhi-32.

ABC Colony
Sahadra, Delhi-32

July 5, 20...

The Editor
The Hindustan Times
K.G. Marg, New Delhi

Subject : Polluted Yamuna

Sir

This is with reference to the article *Overpolluted Yamuna*, dated June 30 and I strongly feel that Yamuna, which is the main source of water supply to Delhi, is in a very sorry state.

The Yamuna has been neglected and no longer enjoys the status of a revered river which it enjoyed a few years ago. Domestic waste and all type of garbage is dumped into the waters of the Yamuna. Near the banks of the Yamuna, many settlements have mushroomed and people from these settlements wash their clothes in this river, thereby adding to the pollution further. Also, the carcasses of animals are disposed of in the Yamuna. The revered river has become murky because of effluents which are dumped into the river,

Time has come to take some preventive measures so that the further deterioration of the situation is checked. Some concerted efforts should be initiated immediately to save the Yamuna which provides a large percentage of its treated water to the people of Delhi and is considered the lifeline of Delhi.

The concerned authorities should take immediate steps to save this lifeline before it dries up or is polluted to an extent from which the retrieval will be impossible.

Thanking you

Yours truly

Rahul

A concerned Delhiite

Write a letter to the Editor of a newspaper expressing your concern about the nuisance of beggars in Delhi, requesting authorities to put a permanent ban on beggary.

G-68 Saket

New Delhi-110017

March 8, 20...

Subject : The Menace of Beggary

The Editor

The Times of India

Bahadur Shah Zafar Marg

New Delhi-110002

Sir

Through the columns of your esteemed daily, I wish to draw the attention of the concerned authorities to a long standing problem of beggary in the capital of India, as this problem has assumed alarming proportions. Earlier, the problem of beggary was confined only to a few who could not work or were crippled or handicapped.

Now beggary seems to have become a regular profession as many able-bodied persons and children are pushed into this trade, as can be seen everywhere. Most of these so-called beggars are professional pick-pockets and thieves, as many incidents of chain-snatching and purse-lifting are reported at the red lights and crossings.

Many anti-social elements have donned the robes of beggars to escape vigilance and hit their targets at opportune time. If not checked immediately, this problem may assume alarming proportions.

It is high time for the concerned authorities to consider this menace seriously and initiate steps to put a permanent ban on this menace in Delhi.

Thanking you

Yours truly
Madan Lal

Write a letter to the Editor of a newspaper expressing your concern about the permission granted by the government for construction of a building block on an open green piece of land near your neighbourhood.

A-18, Anupam Apartments
Saket, New Delhi

26th January, 20...

The Editor
City Observer
K.G. Marg
New Delhi-110001

Subject : Construction on Green Piece of Land

Sir

Kindly allow me to express my shock at the grant of permission by the authorities for constructing a building block in the open green piece of land near the J-block of Saket in South Delhi.

The piece of land on which the proposed construction is likely to begin soon is full of natural greenery and also the habitat of many birds. Rather, it is the only breathing place for the J-block residents and also the nearby blocks. This place must be preserved to maintain the ecological balance of the surrounding areas and should not be converted for residential or commercial purposes.

As Delhi is already an overpopulated, over-congested and polluted city, whatever the green patches are left, should be left as they are.

I therefore request the concerned authorities, through the columns of your esteemed newspaper that they should review their decision and leave this green piece of land untouched. The proposed construction can be carried out at some other site which may not disturb the ecological balance.

Thanking you

Yours truly

C.P. Thakur

Write a letter to the Editor of a local daily of your area expressing your concern about a bad piece of road that needs immediate repair.

3 Anupam Road
Saket, New Delhi

26 April 20...

The Editor
City Observer
K.G. Marg
New Delhi

Sir

I have the following for your kind consideration and publication in your esteemed daily.

For the last two months Anupam Road has become virtually impassable. The heavy rains have broken up the surface badly. When the street lights are off or on a dark night it is very dangerous for the vehicles to move on this road.

Besides, there are piles of road metal on both sides of the road which leave no room in the middle of the road.

Personal requests and private appeals to the Municipality have borne no fruit and hence there is need for a little publicity, as the local residents and public in general have been inconvenienced greatly and unless public pressure is mounted, the concerned authorities do not seem to want to repair the road.

Thanking you

Yours truly

Rakesh

Write a letter to the Editor, the Times of India on reckless driving.

243, Rajouri Garden
New Delhi

August 7, 20...

The Editor
The Times of India
Bahadur Shah Jafar Marg
New Delhi

Subject : Reckless Driving

Sir

Through your esteemed daily, I would like to draw the attention of the concerned authorities that it is high time proper steps be initiated to put a check on the reckless driving of motorcars and other vehicles on the roads in Delhi.

Two hundred and thirty deaths were reported due to accidents during the last six months. Many children were the victims of rash and reckless driving. Old men, women and children have lost lives while crossing the roads. Even in the narrow roads and lanes of our city, the motorists drive rash, paying no heed to safety norms and caring little for others' lives.

Although there are regulations regarding the speed limits, the drivers pay scant heed to them. Unless the safety rules are strictly enforced and erring drivers are given stringent punishment, we cannot expect any improvement in the existing state of affairs.

Sometimes, the traffic police seem to take no notice of the offenders and at others they let off the offenders after accepting bribe. This gives further encouragement to the offenders who are sure that they can escape punishment by greasing the palms of the corrupt traffic policemen.

The public must bring pressure to bear upon the senior policemen and authorities to put a check on reckless driving, otherwise the death rate due to accidents is sure to rise.

Thanking you

Yours truly

Sohan

Write a letter to the Editor of a newspaper about the frequent breakdown of electricity in your locality.

2/97 Govindpuri
Kalkaji, New Delhi

June 26, 20...

The Editor
The Hindustan Times
K.G. Marg
New Delhi

Subject : Erratic Power Supply

Sir

Through the columns of your esteemed newspaper, I would like to draw the attention of the electricity authority (BSES) regarding the frequent breakdown of electricity in Govindpuri area.

There has been frequent breakdown of electricity in our area and the whole place is thrown into complete darkness. Sometimes the electricity supply is not restored for hours which leads to a great inconvenience, especially for the weak and old persons and students who face great difficulty in their studies. June is the hottest month and people have to sweat it out even when they are at their homes after the work. At times the electricity is not available the whole night and any one can imagine the nightmare the residents of this area undergo.

The matter has been reported to the concerned officials of the BSES but it has had no effect and all the complaints have fallen on the deaf ears of the officials. Through your newspaper, it is hoped, that the higher officials of BSES wake themselves and relieve the residents of Govindpuri from this unbearable torture.

Thanking you

Yours truly

Gaitri

for residents of Govindpuri

Write a letter to the Editor of a newspaper expressing your concern about the deteriorating discipline among the students.

D-248, Lajwanti Garden

New Delhi

26th March 20...

The Editor

The Hindustan Times

16-18 K.G. Marg

New Delhi

Sub. : Deteriorating Discipline

Sir

I have the following for your consideration and publication in your esteemed daily.

In recent times, the problem of deteriorating discipline has become the concern of the whole nation. At the slightest offence, the young people lead processions and their unruly mobs indulge in arson and looting. They destroy public and private property. Today, the students have little sense of responsibility, reverence to elders, love for orderliness and dedication to duty.

Some put the entire blame on the students, some blame teachers, while others blame the system of education for this state of affairs. It is really unfortunate that the future makers of India are indisciplined and unruly.

We cannot put the entire blame on students and should try to get to the root of the problem and find some permanent solution. In the modern age of economic stresses, parents have no time to devote to the upbringing of their children. Students are, therefore, ignorant of elementary virtues. In most of the schools too, students do not find congenial atmosphere for the cultivation of discipline. The classes are overcrowded and so no sweet accord between the teacher and the taught exists.

Also, our system of education has become outmoded and obsolete and has outlived its utility. It does not prepare a student for any vocation and the student is haunted by the ghost of unemployment. In fact, our system of education has no aim, nor does it incorporate any spiritual or ethical values.

Thanking you

Yours truly

Rastogi

Write a letter to the Editor of a newspaper about insufficient number of buses on a particular route which causes inconvenience to the commuters.

229-Jasola, Sarita Vihar
New Delhi-110005
August 5, 20...

The Editor
The Hindustan Times
K.G. Marg
New Delhi-110001

Subject : Insufficient Nos. of Buses

Sir

I would like to draw the attention of the concerned authorities about the number of buses on Route No. 377.

During the peak hours, it is very difficult to board the bus route No. 377 plying between Jasola and Nehru Place. There is a heavy rush of passengers on this route and especially during the peak hours in the morning and evening when many commuters have to reach their office and back home after the office hours.

The buses get jam packed at the starting point itself and there is a mad rush to get into the bus afterwards. Old persons, women and children have to face a lot of inconvenience while getting into the bus. Not to talk of getting a seat, even room to stand is hardly available.

I therefore request you to kindly publish the above in the columns of your esteemed daily so that the concerned authorities may initiate action to increase the number of buses on this route.

Thanking you

Yours truly

Salaria

Write a letter to the Editor of the Times of India about the clashing dates of the JEE (IIT) and Haryana Combined Engineering Test.

A-38, Kirti Nagar
New Delhi

July 13, 20...

The Editor
The Times of India
Bahadur Shah Zafar Marg
New Delhi-110002

Subject : Clashing Dates

Sir

I have the following for your kind consideration and publication in the columns of your esteemed daily.

The dates of Examination of the Joint Entrance Examination JEE of IIT and the Haryana Combined Engineering Test are clashing for 13th and 15th August as per the datesheets issued last week.

As many students are going to appear in both the examinations, there is an urgent need to change the dates. If the dates of examinations are not changed suitably, many examinees will have to face a great inconvenience as they will be deprived of the opportunity of appearing in both the examinations.

It is hoped that the concerned authorities will look into this lapse and alter the dates accordingly.

Thanking you

Yours truly

K.L. Kalra

You are a resident of Delhi. After reading the following newspaper article, you write a letter to the Editor of a local newspaper, giving your strong views on the

disadvantages of this project and making an appeal to the government to reconsider its decision.

New Delhi : September 18 Delhi Development Authority has decided to build houses on an 8-acre plot of land which was previously reserved for a sports stadium. This is prime land and the project will provide housing for 4,000 families. This project is likely to be completed by 2007. However, it is facing a stiff opposition from sports lovers.

The Editor
The Hindustan Times
K.G. Marg
New Delhi-110001
September 22, 20...
Subject : Housing Project on Prime Land
Sir

I have read an article in a newspaper that Delhi Development Authority has decided to build 4,000 houses on a piece of land which was previously reserved for building a sports stadium. I am expressing my deep sense of anguish against this decision.

We have seen the poor performance of our sportsmen in the Olympic Games. India stands very poorly at the sports field at international level. We fail to groom our sportsmen from the beginning as is done in other countries. The hopes of a stadium in Delhi could have provided inspiration to budding sportsmen. But this decision of the DDA has dampened the spirits of the sports lovers. Many Indian sportsmen have expressed their displeasure at this move.

I therefore appeal to the DDA to review its decision and build a stadium at this place.

Thanking you
Yours truly
Javed

You read a report in a leading daily how a woman was tortured for not bringing enough dowry. Write a letter to the Editor of the local daily expressing your anguish and horror at such cruel treatment.

The Editor
The Hindustan Times
K.G. Marg
New Delhi-110001

September 20, 20...

Subject : Dowry Brutality

Sir

It was really shocking to read about the inhuman treatment meted out to a woman who had failed to bring sufficient dowry.

Women are still treated like slaves in our society which is the so-called civilised society. This woman was even chained to the bed and not given food for three days. One's blood curdles on reading such news. People have started stooping to any degree just for monetary gains. The pain and agony these hapless women undergo is beyond one's imagination. Earlier also there have been reports of women being harassed and tortured for not bringing sufficient dowry.

This is really inhuman and the avaricious in-laws should be given stringent punishment against this cruelty against human beings. It is hoped that good sense will prevail and human beings will learn in this civilised society, to treat other human beings with love and affection.

Thanking you
Yours truly
Kakaria

CHAPTER 7

COMPREHENSION

SOLVED EXERCISES

PASSAGE 1

Read the given passage and answer the questions that follow :

Socrates was frank and fearless. His outspoken remarks annoyed a number of people. He pricked the pride of many and hurt the vanity of many more. He told those who claimed to be wise and learned that they were cruel and ignorant. His free and frank talk gave him many enemies. Some considered him a crazy person who could stand for a day and night lost in his own thoughts. When he said that he had heard voices and visions, they mistook him for a mad man. Aristophanes, the great dramatist, has presented Socrates in his drama 'The Clouds' as a half crazy old man who corrupts young men of the town. But there were many who admired him and followed him as his disciples in search of truth and wisdom. Among them was Plato, the great philosopher who has revealed the living Socrates in his dialogues.

QUESTIONS

Exercise 1

1. Why was Socrates unpopular during his life time ?
2. What did his enemies think about him ?
3. What is the picture of Socrates presented by Aristophanes in his drama, 'The Clouds' ?

4. How did Socrates's disciples regard him ?
5. Who was Plato ? What did he do for Socrates ?

Exercise 2

Put a Tick Mark (✓) against the true statement and Cross Mark (✗) against the false statement :

1. Many people liked Socrates because he was frank and outspoken in his utterances.
2. Because of his frank speech, Socrates hurt the ego of many persons.
3. Many persons were of the view that Socrates was insane.
4. Aristophanes, in his drama 'The Clouds' has admired Socrates.
5. The great philosopher, Plato, in his dialogues has also criticised Socrates.
6. Socrates wrote the drama 'The Clouds'.
7. Those who admired Socrates became his disciples.
8. Socrates won more enemies than friends because of his frank and fearless talk.

Exercise 3

Write the part of speech of the Italicised words in the following sentences :

1. His *outspoken* remarks *annoyed* a number of people.
2. *When* he said that he had *heard* voices and *visions,* they *mistook him* for a *mad* man.
3. But there were *many* who admired him *and* followed him as his disciples in search of *truth and wisdom.*

Exercise 4

Write the Synonyms of the following words :

1. cruel	2. admired	3. enemies
4. frank	5. truth	6. wise
7. fearless	8. great	

Exercise 5

Use the following words in sentences of your own :

1. visions
2. dramatist
3. corrupts
4. annoyed
5. wisdom
6. hurt
7. vanity
8. revealed

Exercise 6

Fill in the blanks / complete the sentences in the following:

1. A number of people were annoyed by .... remarks.
2. Socrates told those who claimed to be wise and learned that they were :

   (i) ....

   (ii) ....
3. His free and frank talk gave him ....
4. But there were many .... admired him and .... as his disciples .... wisdom.

Exercise 7

Change the voice of the following sentences :

1. His outspoken remarks annoyed a number of people.
2. He pricked the pride of many and hurt the vanity of many more.

ANSWERS

Exercise 1

1. Socrates was unpopular during his life time because he often offended people with his free and frank talk.
2. His enemies thought him to be a crazy person who could stand for a day and night lost in his own thoughts.
3. In his drama 'The Clouds', Aristophanes has presented Socrates as a half-crazy old man.

4. His disciples admired Socrates and followed him in search of truth and wisdom.
5. Plato was a great philosopher who revealed the living Socrates in his dialogues.

Exercise 2

1. (✗)	2. (✓)	3. (✓)	4. (✗)
5. (✗)	6. (✗)	7. (✓)	8. (✓)

Exercise 3

1. outspoken	Adjective
annoyed	Verb
2. when	Conjunction
heard	Verb
visions	Noun
mistook	Verb
him	Pronoun
mad	Adjective
3. many	Pronoun
and	Conjunction
truth	Noun
and	Conjunction
wisdom	Noun

Exercise 4

Word	*Synonym*
1. cruel	causing suffering
2. admired	praised
3. enemies	foes
4. frank	outspoken
5. truth	reality
6. wise	prudent
7. fearless	brave
8. great	important/big

Exercise 5

1. He saw many *visions* of his childhood in his dreams.
2. Shakespeare was a great English *dramatist*.
3. A villain *corrupts* the minds of good persons.
4. The principal was *annoyed* with the students.
5. His *wisdom* has won him many friends.
6. You should not *hurt* his feelings.
7. No one likes her for her *vanity*.
8. The witness *revealed* the secrets to the judge.

Exercise 6

1. his outspoken
2. (i) cruel, (ii) ignorant
3. many enemies
4. (i) who, (ii) followed him, (iii) in search of truth and.

Exercise 7

1. A number of people were annoyed by his outspoken remarks.
2. The pride of many was pricked and the vanity of many more was hurt by him.

PASSAGE 2

In every country people imagine that they are the best and the cleverest and the others are not so good as they are. The Englishman thinks that he and his country are the best. The Frenchman is very proud of France and everything French. The Germans and Italians think no end of their countries and many Indians imagine that India is in many ways the greatest country in the world. This all is conceit. Everybody wants to think well of himself and his country. But in reality, there is no person who has not got some good in him and some bad. In the same way there is no country which is not partly good and partly bad. We must take the good whenever we find it and try to remove the bad wherever it may be. We are, of course, most concerned with our country — India. Unfortunately, it is not in a very good condition today and most of our people are very poor and miserable. They have no pleasure in their lives. We must find out how we can make them happy. We have to see what is good in our own ways and customs and try to keep it, and whatever is bad should be thrown away. If we find anything good in other countries, we should certainly take it.

QUESTIONS

Exercise 1

1. What constitutes conceit ?
2. What should be our attitude towards other countries ?
3. What is the present condition of India ?
4. Are all countries good and perfect ?
5. Write three sentences expressing your agreement or disagreement with the views expressed in the passage.

Exercise 2

Write the part of speech of the Italicised words in the following sentences :

1. The Englishman *thinks that* he and his country are the *best*.
2. In the *same* way there is no *country* which is not *partly* good and partly bad.
3. *We* must find out *how* we can *make* them happy.

Exercise 3

Change the following words to Abstract Nouns :

1. imagine 2. proud 3. remove
4. try 5. happy 6. poor

Exercise 4

Use the following words in sentences of your own :

1. proud 2. conceit 3. pleasure
4. certainly 5. reality

Exercise 5

Write the Synonyms of the following words :

1. conceit 2. miserable 3. customs

Exercise 6

Complete the Degrees of comparison in the following blanks :

	Positive	*Comparative*	*Superlative*
1.	....	....	best
2.	....	....	most
3.	....	....	cleverest
4.	....	....	greatest
5.	Happy	....	....
6.	Bad	....	....

ANSWERS

Exercise 1

1. Most people think that they are the best and the cleverest. They think that their country is the greatest country in the world.
2. We should approach other countries with understanding. We should take the good wherever we find it. We should try to remove the bad wherever it may be.
3. The present condition of India is bad. Most of its people are poor and miserable. They have no joys in their lives.
4. No, all countries are not good and perfect. Every country has some good as well as some bad.
5. We should not think that we are the best people in the world. We should take the good wherever we find it. We should approach the other people with understanding.

Exercise 2

1.	thinks	Verb
	that	Conjunction
	best	Adjective
2.	same	Adjective
	country	Noun
	partly	Adverb
3.	we	Pronoun
	how	Conjunction
	make	Verb

Exercise 3

1. imagination 2. pride 3. removal
4. trial 5. happiness 6. poverty

Exercise 4

1. We should be *proud* of our country.
2. She is disliked for her *conceit*.
3. It is a *pleasure* to meet you after a long time.
4. He will *certainly* report in office on time.
5. *Reality* of life is understood by all of us with the passage of time.

Exercise 5

1. vanity 2. pitiable
3. rituals/usual practices

Exercise 6

	Positive	*Comparative*	*Sup lative*
1.	Good	better	best
2.	Much	more	most
3.	Clever	cleverer	cleverest
4.	Great	greater	greatest
5.	Happy	happier	happiest
6.	Bad	worse	worst

PASSAGE 3

Unemployment in India is neither a bogey nor a red-herring. It is something real and living, which is not going to vanish from our midst soon. Unemployment and underemployment in rural areas, among the educated as well as uneducated, have become endemic. What the much heralded Jawahar Rozgar Yojna sets out to do is merely attempting a 'first aid' job on a gaping wound. Fifty to hundred days' work in a year to at least one member from each rural family living below the poverty line at less than the prevailing wage rate is all the JRY's target. The problem is, however, much too pervasive and ugly.

Rural living is still like flying on a mono plane. If the single engine shuts off due to malfunctioning or bird hit, the high flier hurtles down to crash into a deep heap. Droughts and floods do the same to the rural dweller who has little income other than what he gets from the land, either as a self-employee or wage earner. Plop, he falls into an ocean of hunger and debt from which rescue is most difficult, if not well-nigh impossible. Even without a natural calamity, the life of large numbers of village people is very gruelling. A solution may be : create more jobs. Better farming, culminating in green revolution of a sort in selected areas, has generated some additional employment. But a complete and enduring solution can come only from the large and widespread use of essential goods and services in rural homes which will give work to millions and millions of idle hands.

Whether we mourn the lack of political will or financial constraints, the journey does not look a will–o' the wisp. What we need to tread on a charted or uncharted course is the nation's will to stop the drain from villages to towns and cities to save itself the shame of letting urban slums mushroom.

QUESTIONS

Exercise 1

1. What is the author's opinion about unemployment in India ?

2. What is the target of Jawahar Rozgar Yojna ?
3. What does the author mean when he says that rural living is still like flying on a monoplane ?
4. Suggest two measures which can help the rural people solve the problem of unemployment to some extent.
5. Why are the urban slums mushrooming everyday ?

Exercise 2

Fill in the blanks in the following sentences :

1. Unemployment in India is neither .... nor ....
2. What the much heralded JRY sets out to do is .... wound.
3. Rural living is still like ....
4. The life of a large number of village people is very gruelling even ....
5. The solution to the problem of village people may be :
   (a) To create more jobs.
   (b) ....
6. There are two reasons for the sufferings of the rural people :
   (a) ....
   (b) Financial constraints
7. We can prevent the urban slums from mushrooming if ....

Exercise 3

Put a Tick mark (✓) against the true statement and a Cross mark (X) against the false statement :

1. There is hope that unemployment will vanish from our midst soon.
2. The targets of Jawahar Rozgar Yojna are sufficient to solve the problem of unemployment.

3. The problem of unemployment is too serious for the JRY to solve.
4. Natural calamities such as floods and droughts aggravate the problems of people living in rural areas.
5. Prevention of natural calamities will solve all the problems of people living in rural areas.
6. A complete and enduring solution to the rural unemployment can come only from the large and widespread use of essential goods and services.
7. Lack of political will and financial constraints are also responsible for the problems of rural people.
8. The mushrooming of urban slums can be checked if there is a stop in the drain from villages to towns and cities.

Exercise 4

(A) *Tick the correct part of speech of the Italicised words :*

1. Rural *living* is still like flying on a mono plane.
   (a) Verb (b) Noun (c) Adjective
2. Whether we *mourn* the lack of political will or financial constraints.
   (a) Noun (b) Verb (c) Adverb
3. *If* the single engine shuts off due to malfunctioning.
4. The problem is, however, much too pervasive and *ugly*.

(B) *Write the textual words for the following meanings :*

1. Disappear (Para I)
2. Resulting into (Para II)
3. Lasting (Para II)
4. Existing (Para I)
5. Stops functioning (Para II)

(C) *Write the Antonyms of the following words :*

1. soon 2. employment 3. educated
4. poverty 5. rural

(D) *Use the following words in sentences of your own :*

1. Midst 2. At least 3. Gruelling
4. Lack

(E) *Use 'work' both as* **Noun** *and* **Verb** *in two different sentences :*

(F) *Do as directed :*

1. Droughts and floods do the same to the rural dweller. Change the sentence into Passive Voice.
2. Create more jobs. Change the sentence into Passive Voice.
3. Dweller, poverty, education Change the above words to Verbs.
4. Vanish, complete, grow. Change the above words to Nouns.

ANSWERS

Exercise 1

1. The author is of the view that unemployment in India is something real and living which is not going to disappear from our midst soon.
2. The target of Jawahar Rozgar Yojna is to provide fifty to hundred days' work in a year to at least one member from each rural family living below the poverty line at less than the prevailing wage rate.
3. The author means that people living in rural areas who are poor are fully dependent on the income from land either as self-employees or wage earners. If for some reason this source of income fails, they have nothing else to depend on.
4. Creation of more jobs and better farming can help the rural people solve the problem of unemployment to some extent.

5. The urban slums are mushrooming everyday because more and more people from rural areas come to towns and cities in search of employment.

Exercise 2

1. (i) a bogey (ii) a red herring
2. merely attempting a 'first aid' job on a gaping.
3. flying on a monoplane.
4. Without a natural calamity.
5. (b) Large and widespread use of essential goods and services in rural homes.
6. (a) The lack of political will.
7. we stop the drain from villages to towns and cities.

Exercise 3

1. (✗)	2. (✗)	3. (✓)	4. (✓)
5. (✗)	6. (✓)	7. (✓)	8. (✓)

Exercise 4

(A) 1. Noun 2. Verb
3. Conjunction 4. Adjective

(B) 1. vanish 2. culminating
3. enduring 4. prevailing
5. malfunctioning

(C) 1. late 2. unemployment
3. uneducated 4. riches
5. urban

(D) 1. Poverty may not vanish from our *midst* soon.
2. You should *at least* respect your parents.
3. We were assigned a *gruelling* task.
4. *Lack* of knowledge may lead to problems.

(E) Work : Noun — Your *work* was appreciated by everyone.

Verb — You must *work* hard or starve.

(F) 1. The same is done to the rural dweller by droughts and floods.

2. Let more jobs be created.
3. (1) dwell (2) impoverish (3) educate
4. (1) vanishment (2) completion (3) growth

PASSAGE 4

Chess is one of oldest known indoor games of mankind. Played all over the world, its addictive appeal to the young and the old does not necessitate further elaboration. Chess is known to have held a remarkable sway over its lovers, who according to a folklore, lost even their kingdoms owing to their preoccupation with it. Undoubtedly, a great stimulant for the human mind, like magic, it keeps players spellbound for hours.

After much painstaking research, it is concluded that Chess originated in India, though China too is a contender for this claim. But much evidence points to India as the land of its origin. It is difficult to associate the invention of chess with some specific time period in history simply because of data. Hindu mythology believes that Queen Mandodari, the wife of Ravana, contributed significantly to the invention of chess. Apparently, it was conceived as a pastime to occupy oneself in the intervals between frequently- fought wars. It is also quite likely that it was evolved by women to keep themselves busy while their spouses were away in the battle-field.

The original name of Chess was 'Chaturanga' i.e., four 'Chaturangas' or parts of any army comprising elephants, horses, chariots and foot soldiers. A different version of the origin of Chess is that the game was invented by someone in north-west India around the 5th century A.D. The inventor demanded from the local king a very peculiar reward. Though the king was prepared to give a very handsome reward, the inventor asked for something apparently ridiculous. He sought that every square on the chess board be covered in such a manner that to start with one grain he placed on the first square, its double on the second square, again its double on the third square and so on with continuous doubling of grain in every subsequent square till the last square was filled. This seemingly simple request when complied with, turned out to be a Herculian task as the total number of grains required amounted to a staggering figure.

QUESTIONS

Exercise 1

1. In which country did Chess originate ?
2. What does the Hindu mythology say about the invention of Chess ?
3. Give two possible reasons, as mentioned by the author, why Chess was invented.
4. What reward did the inventor of Chess, according to the second version, demand ?

Exercise 2

Put a Tick Mark (✓) against the true statement and a Cross Mark (X) against the false statement.

1. Chess is one of the oldest outdoor games of mankind.
2. Chess is played only in the north-east part of the world.
3. Chess can keep players spell-bound for hours.
4. Both India and China claim that Chess originated in their countries.
5. It is easy to associate the invention of Chess with specific time period in history simply because all data are available.
6. Mandodari was the mother of king Ravana.
7. Chess was conceived as a pastime to occupy oneself in the intervals between frequently-fought wars.
8. A different version of the origin of Chess is that the game was invented by someone in north-west India around 2nd century A.D.

Exercise 3

Tick the correct part of speech of the Italicised words in the following sentences :

1. Chess is one of the *oldest* known indoor games of mankind.
   (a) Noun (b) Adjective (c) Adverb
2. Undoubtedly, a great stimulant for the *human* mind.
   (a) Noun (b) Adjective (c) Pronoun
3. After much *painstaking* research, it is concluded that chess originated in India.
   (a) Adjective (b) Verb (c) Noun
4. Hindu mythology believes that Queen Mandodari, the wife of Ravana, contributed *significantly* to the invention of Chess.
   (a) Verb (b) Adjective (c) Adverb
5. The *original* name of Chess was 'Chaturanga'.
   (a) Verb (b) Preposition (c) Adjective
6. A different version of the *origin* of Chess is that the game was invented by someone in north-west India.
   (a) Verb (b) Noun (c) Interjection

Exercise 4

(A) *Use the following words in sentences of your own :*

(i) conceived (ii) pastime
(iii) spellbound (iv) spouses

(B) *Write the textual words for the following meanings :*

(i) wonderful (Para I)
(ii) inferred (Para II)
(iii) husband and wife (Para II)
(iv) obviously (Para III)

(C) *Change the following words to Abstract Nouns :*

(i) young (ii) stimulant (iii) difficult
(iv) occupy (v) likely

(D) *Change the following words to Verbs :*

(i) elaboration (ii) origin
(iii) preoccupation (iv) ridiculous

(E) *Change the voice of the following sentences :*

(i) The inventor demanded from the local king a very peculiar reward.

(ii) It keeps players spellbound for hours.

ANSWERS

Exercise 1

1. Chess originated in India.
2. The Hindu mythology says about the invention of chess that queen Mandodari, the wife of Ravana, contributed significantly to the invention of chess.
3. Chess was invented as a pastime to occupy oneself in the intervals between wars. Secondly, it is also quite likely that it was started by women to keep themselves busy while their husbands were away in the battle field.
4. He sought that each square on the chess board be covered in such a manner that to start with, one grain be placed on the first square, its double on the second and so on till the last square was filled.

Exercise 2

1. (✗) 2. (✗) 3. (✓) 4. (✓)
5. (✗) 6. (✗) 7. (✓) 8. (✗)

Exercise 3

1. Adjective 2. Adjective 3. Adjective
4. Adverb 5. Adjective 6. Noun

Exercise 4

(A) 1. This idea was *conceived* by him.
2. Reading books is a good *pastime*.
3. I was *spellbound* to see the magician performing his magic.
4. The *spouses* should maintain harmony at home.

(B) (i) remarkable (ii) concluded
(iii) spouses (iv) apparently

(C) (i) youth (ii) stimulation
(iii) difficulty (iv) occupation
(v) likelihood

(D) (i) elaborate (ii) originate
(iii) preoccupy (iv) ridicule

(E) (i) A very peculiar reward was demanded by the inventor from the local king.
(ii) Players are kept spellbound for hours by it.

PASSAGE 5

Gandhiji went to the meeting out of curiosity. He had no other motive. As he sat and listened to the lip service that prince paid to prince, he became uneasy in his chair. At last, he rose in that great assembly of vested interests—a somewhat unknown person — and with the President's permission began to speak on a matter that worried him intensely. He spoke of the police vigilance in honour of the Viceroy and hordes of policemen that swamped the city "Rather are thousands times", he said "than be followed by a pack of policemen".

A hushed assembly turned round to see who this stranger was in their midst. A murmur ran through the whole crowd. On the platform, there was a confusion and prince conferred with prince over the identity of this Mr. Gandhi of whom they had never heard. They were sure he was of no consequence. Only Mrs. Annie Besant who sat on the platform remembered these Kathiawari features as being those of a young man who had recently appeared at the meeting of the Congress — a child in politics, she said to those around her.

Gandhiji finished with the Viceroy and his policy. He then went on to tackle the princes themselves. He told them how empty was their pomp and how unimportant they really were in India. The President, unaccustomed to such gross impoliteness — for the princes never spoke to each other except with utmost courtesy — did not know how to handle the situation. It was unprecedented and had come as a complete surprise to everyone. But this unknown insignificant little man was carrying the crowd with him. They cheered him as he spoke their thoughts. If only they could think freely and speak like him without fear ! Those on the platform were too dumb-founded to do or say anything. Eventually the President was seen to get up and leave. He was followed by the other princes.

QUESTIONS

Exercise 1

1. What was the reaction of Mr. Gandhi's remarks about the Viceroy and his police guard ?
2. What did Gandhi tell the princes ?
3. How did the crowd react to Gandhi's speech ?
4. What happened in the end ?

Exercise 2

Put a Tick Mark (✓) against the true statement and a Cross Mark (✗) against the false statement :

1. Gandhi remained calm and composed throughout the meeting.
2. Gandhi was known to most of the persons who had come to attend the meeting.
3. Mrs. Annie Besant declared that Gandhi was a child in politics.
4. Gandhi spoke about the Viceroy and his policy and about princes.
5. The princes used to speak discourteously to each other.
6. The crowd in the meeting liked Gandhi's speech and cheered him.
7. The crowd present in the meeting also thought freely and spoke like Gandhi without fear.

8. The men on the platform were indifferent to Gandhi's speech.
9. Gandhi declared in the meeting that the pomp of the Viceroy and others was empty and that they were really unimportant people in India.
10. The President and princes ridiculed the speech of Gandhiji.

Exercise 3

Tick the correct part of speech of the Italicised words :

1. Gandhiji went to the meeting out of *curiosity*.
   (a) Noun (b) Verb (c) Adverb
2. Gandhiji *finished* with the Viceroy and his policy.
   (a) Pronoun (b) Verb (c) Adverb
3. A *hushed* assembly turned *round* to see
   (i) (a) Verb (b) Conjunction (c) Adjective
   (ii) (a) Noun (b) Verb (c) Adverb
4. *He* spoke their thoughts.
   (a) Interjection (b) Verb (c) Pronoun
5. *On* the platform there was confusion.
   (a) Verb (b) Adjective (c) Preposition
6. On the platform there was confusion *and* prince *conferred* with prince over the identity of this Mr. Gandhi.
   (i) (a) Preposition (b) Conjunction (c) Adverb
   (ii) (a) Verb (b) Adverb (c) Adjective

Exercise 4

(A) *Change the following words to Nouns :*

(1) uneasy (2) speak (3) worried
(4) empty (5) except (6) think

(B) *Change the following words to Adjectives :*

(1) curiosity (2) freely (3) fear
(4) eventually (5) vigilance (6) honour

(C) *Write the Antonyms of the following words :*

(1) uneasy	(2) intensely	(3) remembered
(4) began	(5) great	(6) impoliteness

(D) *Do as directed :*

1. Gandhiji went to this meeting out of curiosity. Write the above sentence as 'Complex' sentence.
2. He told them how empty was their pomp. Rewrite as 'simple' sentence.
3. They cheered him.
   Change the above sentence to Passive Voice.
4. They were sure he was of no consequence.
   Change the above sentence to 'Compound' sentence.
5. Those on the platform were to dumb-founded to do or say anything.
   Rewrite the sentence using 'so .... that' in place of 'too — to'.

ANSWERS

Exercise 1

1. A tongue-tied assembly turned round to see this stranger (Gandhiji) among them. A murmur ran through the whole crowd. Even on the stage, there was confusion.
2. Gandhiji told the princes their pomp was quite empty. They were quite unimportant in the India that mattered.
3. The crowd was happy as Gandhiji spoke their thoughts. They cheered him.
4. In the end, the President was seen getting up and leaving. He was followed by the other princes.

Exercise 2

1. (✗)	2. (✗)	3. (✓)	4. (✓)
5. (✗)	6. (✓)	7. (✗)	8. (✗)
9. (✓)	10. (✗)		

Exercise 3

1. Noun
2. Verb
3. (i) Adjective (ii) Adverb
4. Pronoun
5. Preposition
6. (i) Conjunction (ii) Verb

Exercise 4

(A) (1) uneasiness (2) speech
(3) worry (4) emptiness
(5) exception (6) thought

(B) (1) curious (2) free
(3) fearful/fearsome (4) eventual
(5) vigilant (6) honourable

(C) (1) comfortable (2) lightly
(3) forgot (4) stopped
(5) small (6) politeness

(D) 1. Gandhiji went to this meeting as he was curious.
2. He told them about their pomp being empty.
3. He was cheered by them.
4. He was of no consequence and they were sure of it.
5. Those on the platform were so dumb-founded that they could not do or say anything.

Exercises for Practice

PASSAGE 1

Read the passage carefully and answer the questions that follow :

Should the leader lead from the front or the back ? The best leader leads from behind when things are going on course. By doing this, he not only becomes a follower but allows the followers to lead during easier times, thereby giving ample scope for budding leaders to emerge and take initiative. This way he not only conserves his energy but also allows others to vent their energy. This provides ample freedom for the group to take directions which the leader could never have thought about singly.

As long as the movement is going fine, the leader takes a back seat and let things take their own course. A leader is known for his acumen by the things he chooses to leave undone as much as for the things he chooses to do.

He does not wish to control every detail and squander his energy on trivia, but conserves it for more important tasks. He remains in the background as long as he is not required.

A good leader is a democratic leader. He leads by consensus and does not impose his decisions on his subordinates but enlists their support for every decision. He does not come down too harshly on errants, but knows the exact amount of firmness and the tact required for the implementation of task. He does not put a ton of pressure when a kilo will suffice. A good leader is patient with his subordinates for he knows that they may come out with better solutions and may know their particular fields better than him.

The leader brings out the best among his followers by allowing them complete freedom of opinion. He encourages free discussion and open debate on any issue for he knows that the truth is not his private preserve but is arrived at through shared experiences and perceptions.

QUESTIONS

Exercise 1

Answer the following questions :

1. What are the advantages of leading from behind ?

   ....

2. Why does a good leader take a back seat ?

   ....

3. Why doesn't a good leader wish to control every detail ?

....

4. Why is a good leader called democratic leader ?

....

5. How does the quality of being patient help a good leader ?

....

Exercise 2

Put a Tick Mark (✓) against the true statement and a Cross Mark (X) against the false statement :

1. The best leader should always lead from the front. ( )
2. If things are going on well, a good leader leads from behind. ( )
3. A good leader never allows his followers to lead. ( )
4. A good leader gives enough scope to budding leaders to initiate. ( )
5. By not giving ample scope to budding leaders, a good leader may put his energy to the best use. ( )
6. When the movement is going on fine, a good leader takes a back seat and lets things take their course. ( )
7. If a leader chooses to leave things undone, he cannot be called a good leader. ( )
8. A good leader does not desire to control every detail and waste his energy on insignificant things. ( )
9. A good leader is an authoritative leader. ( )
10. A good leader always imposes his decisions on his subordinates. ( )

11. A good leader is always firm and harsh to wrong-doers. ( )
12. A good leader is patient and tactful. ( )
13. A good leader knows how to do the things and how to get the things done. ( )
14. Subordinates may know things better than their leader in certain fields. ( )
15. A good leader never allows free discussion and open debate. ( )

Exercise 3

Complete the following sentences / blanks :

1. The best leader leads from .... when things are going ....
2. By doing so, the best leader not only .... energy but also .... energy.
3. As long as the movement is going fine, the leader .... seat .... course.
4. A leader is known for his .... by the things he chooses .... as much as for the things he chooses to do.
5. A good leader does not wish .... detail and .... his energy on ....
6. As long as a good leader is not required, he remains ....
7. A good leader leads .... and does not .... his decisions on his subordinates.
8. A good leader is .... subordinates, for he knows that they may come out with .... solutions and may .... better than him.
9. A good leader allows his subordinates .... opinion.

10. A good leader .... free discussion and .... on any issue.

Exercise 4

A. *Tick (✓) the correct meanings of the Italicised words from the different choices :*

1. The best leader *leads from behind.*
   (a) walks behind others
   (b) is generally left behind
   (c) controls the things with least interference.
2. Thereby leaving ample scope for *budding leaders* to emerge and take initiative.
   (a) experienced leaders
   (b) highly qualified leaders
   (c) leaders who are in the process of learning.
3. As long as the *movement is going fine.*
   (a) when the leaders are moving fine
   (b) when the leaders' steps are in control
   (c) when the things are going on well.
4. The leader *takes a back seat.*
   (a) sits on the back seat
   (b) is generally not interested in work
   (c) allows others to take control.
5. He does not wish to control every detail and *squander energy on trivia.*
   (a) wastes energy on insignificant things
   (b) conserves his energy for future
   (c) conserves his energy for smaller matters.
6. A good leader is a *democratic leader.*
   (a) belonging to the democratic party
   (b) leader sharing power with others
   (c) leader belonging to a democratic country.
7. A good leader is *patient with his subordinates.*
   (a) shows firmness to his subordinates
   (b) shows perseverance towards his juniors
   (c) is generally sick of his subordinates.

8. He encourages *free discussion and open debate.*
   (a) where no money is involved in discussion
   (b) when all are allowed to give their opinions
   (c) when discussion is limited to non-profit matters.

(B) *Write the Past and Past Participles of the following verbs :*

Present	*Past*	*Past Participle*
1. Lead	....	....
2. Take	....	....
3. Conserve	....	....
4. Emerge	....	....
5. Suffice	....	....

(C) *Form Verbs from the following words :*

Word		**Verb**
1. Leader	:	....
2. Direction	:	....
3. Pressure	:	....
4. Solution	:	....
5. Discussion	:	....

(D) *Write the Antonyms of the following words :*

Word		**Antonym**
1. Ample	:	....
2. Conserve	:	....
3. Follower	:	....
4. Back	:	....
5. Encourages	:	....

(E) *Use the following words / expressions in sentences of your own :*

1. From the front..
2. Emerge..
3. Initiative ....
4. Acumen..
5. Squander ....

(F) *Do as directed :*

1. A good leader is patient with his subordinates. (Rewrite the sentence after using Noun form of 'patient' without changing the meaning.
2. The best leader leads from behind. (Rewrite the sentence making it Negative without changing its meaning)
3. The leader takes a back seat. Change the above sentence into Passive Voice.
4. He encourages free discussion and open debate on any issue. Change the above sentence into Passive Voice.

PASSAGE 2

A queer little animal that one frequently comes across on the Ladakhi uplands is the marmot. About the size of a small spaniel it wears a thick coat of reddish brown or golden coloured fur. A fully grown marmot measures from 24 to 36 inches, body and tail both. The tail, which is bushy, is about one-third of the total length. The marmot seams to be somewhat allied to the squirrel or the mongoose. Locally known as *Drun* or *Drin*, it is the despair of dogs. It has the curious habit of popping up on its hind legs at the entrance to its hole when it sees somebody and uttering shrill, piercing cries. The dog accompanying the passersby runs to catch it. The self confident little creature stands unruffled till the dog is almost upon it. But when it actually gets there, it, at once, drops down into its burrow, to the chagrin of the dog. And soon after, when the disappointed dog is gone away, the marmot pops up again to resume its shrill tantalising cries. Though easy to shoot, the marmot is not usually killed, as it is not of any use. Even its handsomely tinted skin is too coarse and wiry from the furrier's point of view.

The marmot spends the winter in the depths of its burrow. During its long winter slumber, it subsists largely on its accumulated fat. But not entirely; for in autumn, it stocks large quantities of grass and roots in subterranean passages around its burrow for use during the long dreary winter. Accustomed to its long winter slumber, the marmot can withstand hunger for long periods. This created a lot of surprise when some Army drivers brought a marmot from Dras to Srinagar. This writer also went to see this 'large mouse' as it was described. I at once recognised the poor captive from Dras and told its captors so. They were greatly surprised that it had taken nothing for the past six days.

I told them that its 'hunger strike' was in protest against their action in tearing it away from its home and therefore, they should carry it back to its natural habitat. They were,. at first reluctant to do so as one of them wanted to make a fur cap for himself from its skin. But when I told them that its fur was not of much use for the purpose, they agreed to take it back to its home the next morning.

QUESTIONS

Exercise 1

On the basis of your reading of the passage, answer the following questions as briefly as possible. Write your answers in the space provided.

1. Marmot is stated to be too clever to be caught by a dog for two reasons

   (a) ....

   (b) ....

2. Marmot is not at all a game animal. It is because of two reasons. These are :

   (i) the fact that ....

   (ii) and secondly ....

3. Marmot spends the winter in its burrow. Its chief sources of food, then, are
   (i) The ....
   (ii) the stocks of ....
4. The writer told the Army drivers that Marmot 'fur was not of much use for the purpose'; this means that ....
   ....
5. This passage has been titled as 'Marmot' referring to the description of the large mouse. However, this also refers to the fact that the marmot is a game animal. ....

Exercise 2

Put a Tick Mark (✓) against the true statement and a Cross Mark (✗) against the false statement :

1. The tail of the marmot is bushy and is one-fourth of the total length of the marmot. ( )
2. The marmot is the despair and chagrin of the dog. ( )
3. As the marmot is easy to kill, the hunters often shoot it down. ( )
4. The marmot can not tolerate hunger for long periods. ( )
5. The marmot is used to long winter sleep. ( )
6. The Army drivers described the marmot as 'large mouse'. ( )
7. According to the writer, the fur of the marmot is not of much use for making a fur cap. ( )
8. The marmot is found on the Ladakhi upland. ( )

Exercise 3

(A) *Use the following words in sentences of your own :*

1. queer	2. mongoose	3. burrow
4. resume	5. slumber	6. chagrin

(B) *Write the Synonyms of the following words :*

Word	Synonym
1. uttering	....
2. confident	....
3. disappointed	....
4. slumber	....
5. surprised	....

(C) (i) *Change the following words to Nouns :*

1. curious 2. confident 3. resume
4. natural 5. disappointed

(ii) *Change the following words to Verbs :*

1. habit 2. captor 3. thick
4. confident 5. length

(iii) *Change the Voice of the following :*

1. The marmot is not usually killed.
2. It wears a thick coat of reddish brown or golden coloured fur.
3. The marmot can stand hunger for long periods.

(D) *Do as directed :*

(i) A fully grown marmot measures from 24 to 36 inches.
Rewrite the above sentence after using the Noun form of 'measures' without changing the meaning.

(ii) Even its handsomely tinted skin is too coarse and wiry from the furrier's point of view.
Rewrite the sentence after using 'so .... that' expression for 'too coarse'.

PASSAGE 3

A close study of the lives and works of great teachers and high educational dignitaries such as Tagore, Radha-krishnan, Zakir Hussain and Saiydain, indicate that these luminaries, from the very beginning, were committed to high ideals and superior academic norms, which placed the stamp of excellence on their achievements in the field of education. Many of them made noble efforts for strengthening and enriching the educational curricula and programmes and the teacher education courses and in imbuing to education a distinct personality of its own. In fact, they were the cultivated minds and integrated personalities, inspired and infused by the high ideals of our great and ancient heritage, willing and ready to work in the service of the nation. If all teachers follow the path shown by such educational authorities, education is bound to achieve its goal of all-round development.

Education, of which teachers are purveyors, is the sacred instrument for building the nation. Teacher's is the most crucial job of moulding the character of individuals and thereby of shaping the society itself. Education is a medium through which he will direct human energies and human capacities to the advancement of human weal. Upon the nature and character of education imparted by him depends the future of nation. It need not be emphasised that there is a casual relationship between education on the one hand and economic growth and social progress on the other. As teachers alone have to administer this education, one can imagine the colossal responsibility they have of performing this stupendous task.

While they perform this task, they should keep in mind that education is not learning what to do, but becoming the kind of person who knows what to do. Child is not just a learner of history or science. His interests, his aptitude, his habits and everything else which goes towards the make-up of his personality comes within the teacher's purview. Teachers have to produce mentally healthy individuals who have wholesome personalities. Teachers represent the ideals and aspirations of the nation and owe to it the moral and mental accountability of equipping the youth for active participation in the high enterprise of creating a social order which shall dispense equal justice to all and sundry.

As ideal teachers, they have to strive, along with their wards, to build up the nation in conformity with the lofty ideals laid down in our Constitution. This great aim can be realised by effective, brilliant teachers, teachers who are equipped with the training that has a direct bearing on the quality of life in the community, and that will serve as the chief means for the transformation of the society. Such teachers can make their contribution to the building up of a new India — India that is holding fast to the traditional culture of the past and is both forward-looking and future-oriented. It is these teachers alone who can provide, through rich and dynamic education, all that the country needs for its prosperity.

QUESTIONS

Exercise 1

1. *Mention four qualities of Tagore, Radhakrishnan, Zakir Hussain and Saiydain which made them great teachers. Write your answers in the space provided.*

   (a) ....

   (b) ....

   (c) ....

   (d) ....

2. *On the basis of your reading of the passage, answer the following questions as briefly as possible :*

   Tagore, Radhakrishnan, Zakir Hussain etc. are known as great teachers and educationists. There are many reasons for this. However,

   (a) one reason is that ....

   (b) and the other is that ....

These personalities were the cultivated minds because

(c) they ....

(d) and they ....

Education can be used :

(e) to ....

(f) ....

(g) Teachers have a great responsibility because ....

(h) "This aim can be realised by effective, brilliant teachers ..." (para 4) what is the aim ?

....

Teachers' teaching can act as the chief means of

(i) ....

(j) and ....

Exercise 2

Put a Tick Mark (✓) against the true statement and a Cross Mark (X) against the false statement.

1. Great educationists were committed to high ideals and superior academic norms from the very beginning. ( )
2. These educationists were always willing to work in the service of the nation. ( )
3. In fact, teachers are not the purveyors of education. ( )
4. Teachers play the most crucial role of moulding the character of individuals. ( )
5. However, teachers can not do much in shaping the society. ( )
6. Education and economic growth are casually related. ( )
7. Teachers must produce mentally healthy individuals who have wholesome personalities. ( )

8. Child is just a learner of history or science. ( )
9. The quality of life in community is certainly affected by the training imparted by the brilliant teachers. ( )
10. Teachers are not morally and mentally answerable for equipping the youth for active participation in the high enterprise of creating a social order. ( )

Exercise 3

(A) *Find words in the passage, from the paragraphs indicated which mean the opposite of each of the following.*

1. inferior (Para 1)
2. ignoble (Para 1)
3. desecrated (Para 2)
4. immoral (Para 3)
5. backward-looking (Para 4)

(B) *Use the following words in sentences of your own :*

1. superior	2. luminaries	3. academic
4. sacred	5. distinct	6. crucial

(C) *Do as directed :*

(i) Many of them made noble efforts for strengthening and enriching the educational curricula and programmes (change the above sentence into Passive Voice).

(ii) If all teachers follow the path shown by such educational authorities, education is bound to achieve its goal of all-round development.

Rewrite the above sentence beginning with unless ....

(iii) *Change the following words to Nouns :*

1. educational	2. integrated	3. achieve
4. economic	5. brilliant	6. dynamic

(iv) *Change the following words to Verbs :*

1. development	2. education
3. prosperity	4. achievement

CHAPTER 8

TELEGRAMS

Telegram is a quick and cheap mode of communication used by the common man to communicate an important message or an urgent business deal. While drafting a telegram, the following points should be followed :

(i) The Address of the Addressee should be written in block letters.

(ii) The Message should be clear and brief.

(iii) The Message should also be written in block letters.

(iv) The word 'STOP' should be used for a full stop to ensure clarity.

(v) Articles (a, an the), Prepositions and Auxiliaries (helping verbs) can be omitted if clarity is not distorted.

(vi) Complete sentences should not be used.

(vii) Clauses and Phrases should be used.

1. Suresh wrote the following letter to his father. Then he decided to send a telegram instead of the letter. Using relevant information from the letter, write this telegram in the space below, using not more than 20 words :

A-248, Model Town-II
New Delhi

15-7-20...

Dear Papa

I am extremely happy to inform you that I have been selected as Sales Manager in Hindustan Lever Ltd. I am to join my duties on 1st August. As you know, it was my heartiest desire to join this company after I did my MBA. About fifteen candidates were interviewed and I was hopeful of my selection as I was able to influence the Selection Panel of my abilities in sales.

All is well at home. Please write about your welfare. When are you coming home ?

Your loving son

Suresh

<table>
<tr><td colspan="3">INDIAN POST AND TELEGRAPH</td></tr>
<tr><td>Address of the Addressee :</td><td>Name :
Address
Telegraph office :
Tele No. (if any)</td><td>Capt. Sahni
C/o 99 APO</td></tr>
<tr><td>Message :</td><td colspan="2">APPOINTED SALES MANAGER
HINDUSTAN LEVER STOP
JOINING FIRST
AUGUST STOP</td></tr>
<tr><td>Sender's Name :</td><td colspan="2">SURESH</td></tr>
<tr><td colspan="3">(NOT TO BE TELEGRAPHED)</td></tr>
<tr><td>SENDER'S ADDRESS</td><td></td><td>A-248, Model Town II
New Delhi</td></tr>
</table>

2. ***You are Rakesh Sharma, resident of G-67 Saket, New Delhi. You have to attend an interview for the post of Purchase Manager in Mumbai. You will reach Mumbai on 6th at 8 A.M. by Rajdhani Express. Draft a telegram to be sent to your friend with whom you wish to stay for two days.***

INDIAN POST AND TELEGRAPH		
Address of the Addressee :	Name :	SAHIL
	Address	58, NORTH AVENUE MUMBAI
	Telegraph office : Tele No. (if any)	
Message :	INTERVIEW FOR PURCHASE MANAGER STOP REACHING MUMBAI SIXTH AT EIGHT A.M. RAJDHANI EXPRESS STOP WILL STAY TWO DAYS STOP	
Sender's Name :	RAKESH SHARMA	
(NOT TO BE TELEGRAPHED)		
Sender's Address		G-67, Saket New Delhi

3. ***Rohan wrote the following letter to his father. Then he decided to send a telegram instead of the letter. Using relevant information from the letter, draft this telegram in the space below in not more than 20 words.***

St. Paul School Hostel
Shimla
Himachal Pradesh

Dear Papa

I hope everything is fine at home.

You will be glad to know that I have fared very well in my annual examination securing 95% marks. Our school is organising a one-week's historical tour to different places. All my classmates are joining this tour. As I also wish to join it, please allow me to do so and also send Rs. 1000/- for the expenses.

I am not coming home soon but will come home directly from Delhi after we come back from the tour.

My regards to dear mama and love to Chirag.

Your loving son

Rohan

INDIAN POST AND TELEGRAPH		
Address of the Addressee :	Name : Address	PRATAP KOHLI 47, KARNAL ROAD PANIPAT
	Telegraph office : Tele No. (if any)	
Message :	JOINING SCHOOL HISTORICAL TOUR STOP NOT COMING HOME NOW STOP WILL COME AFTER TOUR STOP SEND RUPEES ONE THOUSAND STOP	
Sender's Name :	ROHAN	
(Not to be Telegraphed) Sender's Address		St. Paul School Hostel Shimla

4. *Rajni wrote the following letter to the Secretary, Union Public Service Commission. Then she decided to send a telegram instead of the letter. Using relevant information from the letter, write this telegram in the space below in about 20 words :*

38, Hemkund Colony
New Delhi-110048

3rd July 20...

The Secretary
Union Public Service Commission
Shahjahan Road
New Delhi

Subject : Change of Examination Centre

Sir

I am to appear in the ensuing Civil Service Examination to be held by UPSC, New Delhi. I have been allotted examination centre at Lucknow, though I wrote Delhi as the centre for this examination in the Application Form. I won't be able to leave the station even for one night as my mother-in-law is bed-ridden and my husband is out of station.

Keeping the above circumstances in view, I request you to change my examination centre from Lucknow to Delhi.

Thanking you

Yours faithfully
Rajni
Roll No. 2394808

<table>
<tr><td colspan="3">INDIAN POST AND TELEGRAPH</td></tr>
<tr><td>Address of the
Addressee :</td><td>Name :
Address

Telegraph office :
Tele No. (if any)</td><td>SECRETARY
UPSC, New Delhi</td></tr>
<tr><td>Message :</td><td colspan="2">UNABLE TO TAKE CIVIL SERVICE
EXAM AT LUCKNOW STOP.
PRESSING CIRCUMSTANCES STOP
CHANGE CENTRE TO DELHI STOP</td></tr>
<tr><td>Sender's Name :</td><td colspan="2">Rajni, Roll No. 2394808</td></tr>
<tr><td colspan="3">(Not to be Telegraphed)

Sender's Address   38, HemKund Colony
New Delhi</td></tr>
</table>

5. ***Imagine you are going to Delhi on an urgent work and will stay there for three days. Write a telegram in not more than 20 words to Hotel Merriot, Saket, New Delhi, requesting reservation and confirmation of the same.***

INDIAN POST AND TELEGRAPH		
Address of the Addressee	Name : Address	— HOTEL MERRIOT SAKET NEW DELHI
	Telegraph office : Tele No. (if any)	
Message :	RESERVE ONE BED-ROOM STOP ARRIVING NINE P.M. AUGUST TEN STOP STAYING THREE DAYS STOP CONFIRM	
Sender's Name : RAJAT		
(Not to be Telegraphed)		
Sender's Address		28, AB Colony, Panipat Haryana

6. ***Imagine that your annual examination is over. As you have to attend a cricket coaching camp, you are not going home soon. Write a telegram to your father informing him of the same.***

INDIAN POST AND TELEGRAPH		
Address of the Addressee	Name : Address Telegraph office : Tele No. (if any)	RAKESH 52 CHIRAG ENCLAVE NEW DELHI
Message :	NOT COMING HOME AFTER ANNUAL EXAM STOP ATTENDING CRICKET CAMP TEN DAYS STOP	
Sender's Name :	CHIRAG	
(Not to be Telegraphed) Sender's Address		Belham Boys School Hostel Mussoori

7. ***Imagine that your friend Sonu has qualified for the Civil Services Examination. Send him a telegram congratulating him.***

INDIAN POST AND TELEGRAPH		
Address of the Addressee	Name : Address Telegraph office : Tele No. (if any)	SONU 3, TILAK MARG DEHRADOON
Message :	HEARTIEST CONGRATULATIONS ON QUALIFYING CIVIL SERVICE EXAM STOP	
Sender's Name :	RAJIV	
(Not to be Telegraphed) Sender's Address		3/7 Shastri Nagar Lucknow

8. Suppose you are the Principal of St. Paul School Mathura. You had sent the Examination forms of 20 students of your school to CBSE, New Delhi. Though the examination is due after 10 days, your school has not received the Roll No. slips of these students yet. Write a telegram in not more than 20 words to CBSE, New Delhi for sending the Roll No. slips immediately.

<table>
<tr><th colspan="3">INDIAN POST AND TELEGRAPH</th></tr>
<tr><td>Address of the Addressee</td><td>Name :
Address

Telegraph office :
Tele No. (if any)</td><td>CBSE
CBSE,
NEW DELHI</td></tr>
<tr><td>Message :</td><td colspan="2">SEND ROLL NO. SLIPS OF TWENTY STUDENTS CLASS TEN STOP OUR REFERENCE NO. 238/ADM/20... JANUARY FOURTEEN STOP</td></tr>
<tr><td>Sender's Name :</td><td colspan="2">Principal St. Paul School Mathura</td></tr>
<tr><td colspan="3">(Not to be Telegraphed)

Sender's Address   St. Paul School Mathura</td></tr>
</table>

9. Send a telegram to your friend at Allahabad informing him of your visit to Allahabad and asking him to receive you at the railway station. The telegram (not including the address) should not

exceed 15 words. You are Anil Kumar of 2/97 Govindpuri Kalkaji, New Delhi.

INDIAN POST AND TELEGRAPH		
Address of the Addressee	Name : Address	N. SURI 42, AVENUE ROAD ALLAHABAD
	Telegraph office : Tele No. (if any)	
Message :	REACHING ALLAHABAD BY SANGAM EXPRESS SIXTH MAY STOP RECEIVE AT STATION STOP TO STAY SIX DAYS STOP	
Sender's Name :	Anil Kumar	
(Not to be Telegraphed) Sender's Address		2/97, Govindpuri, Kalkaji New Delhi

10. Your friend has recently undergone a serious operation. Draft a telegram wishing him a speedy recovery.

INDIAN POST AND TELEGRAPH		
Address of the Addressee :	Name : Address : Telegraph office : Tele No. (if any)	S.N. SHARMA 4, TIMARPUR MUMBAI
Message :	SHOCKED TO HEAR OF YOUR SERIOUS OPERATION STOP WISHING YOU SPEEDY RECOVERY STOP	
Sender's Name :	K.L. Soni	
(Not to be Telegraphed) Sender's Address		41, Bungalow Road, Amritsar

EXERCISES FOR PRACTICE

1. You live in a school hostel and plan to join a short trip to the hills with your classmates after the annual examination. Draft a telegram to be sent to your father seeking his permission for the trip and asking him to send you some money for the trip. Also inform him that you will be arriving home after the trip.
2. Imagine you are the General Manager, ABC Electronics Okhla Industrial Area, Phase II. Write a telegram to be sent to Mr. S.K. Gupta informing him that his leave expired on 6th January 20... and he should report for duty immediately.
3. You are the Principal of Laxman Public School, Haus Khas Enclave, New Delhi. The date of interview for the posts of teachers which was fixed for March 8,

stands postponed due to some unavoidable circumstances. The candidates are to be informed accordingly. Draft one such telegram.

4. Imagine you are the Branch Manager of UCO Bank. A theft has taken place in your branch. Draft a telegram in not more than 20 words to the General Manager of the Head office of your Bank reporting this incident.
5. You are Christo residing in 174/P Pushp Vihar, Sector IV, Yamuna Nagar. You wish to visit Delhi in the company of your two friends on the Republic Day and will stay with your cousin residing in A3/230 Janakpuri, New Delhi. Draft a telegram to be sent to him informing about it.
6. Imagine you are the Personnel Manager of Oxford Press, New Delhi. You have fixed an interview for the post of Editor on 22nd August 20.... Due to some unavoidable reasons the interview is to be cancelled. Write one such telegram in not more than 20 words to be sent to the candidates who have been called for the said interview.
7. You are Ashutosh staying in St. Johan's College Hostel, Dehradoon. Your roommate Sunil met with an accident and is admitted in the hospital. Draft a telegram to be sent to his father Mr. R.S. Kohli staying in A-38 Pashchim Vihar, New Delhi informing him about the accident in about 20 words.
8. Draft a telegram to be sent to your father staying at C-1 Lajpat Nagar, informing him that you are not arriving by Jayanti Janta Express as was planned earlier but by Kalka Mail. You will now arrive on 16th May and not on 3rd May.
9. You are Lalit Kumar working in a private firm in Mumbai. You are to go home on leave on 1st August.

But you are unable to do so as you have some urgent work to do. You are not sure of the date of your arrival. Send a telegram to your parents in Kolkata, using not more than 20 words.

10. Mohan wrote the following letter to Sonu. Then he decided to send a telegram instead of the letter. Using relevant information from the letter, write this telegram in the space below, using not more than 20 words.

New Delhi
3rd July 20...

Dear Sonu

My uncle and aunt are visiting Lucknow during the first week of August 20.... They will stay there for three days. Thereafter they will go to Cuttack. They will be arriving in Lucknow by the Rajdhani Express on the morning of August 2. I'd be very grateful if you could arrange a good hotel for three days for them. Could you possibly meet them at the station too ?

Hoping to meet you soon.
Yours affectionately
Mohan

CHAPTER 9

ADVERTISEMENTS

1. On transfer to a far-flung area, you want to dispose of your household effects. Draft a suitable advertisement, in about 20 words for insertion in 'For Sale' column of a newspaper

FOR SALE

A sofa set with Dunlop seats; a dining table with sunmica top with six chairs and a Godrej Almirah are available for immediate sale. Contact 26854704.

2. Prepare a suitable Ad. for the 'Classified Ads' section of a newspaper, for the sale of your Motorcycle.

FOR SALE

A Hero Honda Motor cycle, 2000 December Model, brand new looks, well maintained is for immediate sale. Please contact E-248, Rakesh Nagar, New Delhi, Tele. No. 55679550.

3. You want to sell your collection of rare stamps. Write a suitable advertisement in about 25 words to be printed in a local daily.

FOR SALE

A collection of rare stamps available at throwaway price. Please contact S.K. Chauhan C-42, G.K.-I, New Delhi Phone : 26221583.

4. You have lost your wrist watch in a public park. Write a suitable advertisement for the 'LOST

AND FOUND' column of a newspaper in about 35 words.

LOST AND FOUND

Lost a wrist watch 'HMT' with golden dial and black leather strap on 6th January 20... in Lodhi Gardens, New Delhi. The finder shall be handsomely rewarded. The finder may contact 29252851.

5. You have found a purse containing hundred rupee notes and some important documents in your school. Write a 'Lost and Found' notice for your school notice board.

LOST AND FOUND

Found a purse containing hundred rupee notes and some important documents in the school play ground. The owner may contact the undersigned to collect the purse after giving its particulars and identification mark.

Satinder Singh
X B

6. You have lost a library book issued in your name while travelling in a bus. Prepare a suitable Ad. to be given in the local newspaper.

LOST AND FOUND

Lost a library book titled 'Discovery of India' (by Jawahar Lal Nehru) bearing the stamp of Delhi Public Library, Sarojini Nagar on 4th August 20... in Bus Route No. 750. The finder may please restore the book to Kailash E-48, Nehru Nagar, New Delhi Tele. No. 28923562.

7. You want to let out a flat. Draft a suitable advertisement in about 25 words to be published in the 'To Let' column of a newspaper.

TO LET

A 2 bedroom flat, drawing-cum-dining, ground floor, ideal location, facing park, near the main market is available for rent. Reasonable rent. Please contact 21280234, Rakesh.

8. You are looking for a house on reasonable rent. Prepare a suitable advertisement for publication in a newspaper.

ACCOMMODATION WANTED

Wanted an independent two bed room, drawing-cum-dining room accommodation having car-parking facility, preferably in South Delhi on reasonable rent. Contact 28529286 between 6 P.M. and 9 P.M.

9. Prepare a suitable matrimonial advertisement for publication in a newspaper for a suitable match for your son.

MATRIMONIAL

Suitable alliance sought for a Khatri boy, 28, Manager in a reputed pharmaceutical company drawing Rs. 12,000 p/m. The girl should be beautiful, homely and graduate. Early decent marriage. Caste no bar. Write to Box 38962-CA. The Hindustan Times New Delhi-110001.

10. You are looking for a suitable match for your sister. Prepare a suitable matrimonial advertisement for publication in a newspaper.

MATRIMONIAL

Engineer / Doctor / Executive match from decent family for beautiful Punjabi girl, 25, 152 cm, M.A. Ph.D., lecturer in Delhi University. Early marriage. Dowry-seekers may please excuse. Box 2848, The Hindustan Times, New Delhi-110001.

11. You are the Principal of Rosemary Public School, Janakpuri, New Delhi. You need lady teachers to teach Maths to 12th Class. Draft a suitable advertisement for the 'Situations Vacant' column of a local daily.

SITUATIONS VACANT

Wanted lady teachers, PGT, to teach Maths to 12th Class. Attractive salary for deserving and experienced candidates. Apply with full particulars within fifteen days to the Principal, Rosemary Public School, Janakpuri, New Delhi.

12. You are the Managing Director of ABC Electronics Limited, Okhla Industrial Area, Phase II, New Delhi. You need a competent lady private Secretary for your office. Draft an advertisement to be published in the newspaper.

SITUATIONS VACANT

Wanted a competent lady private Secretary for a Limited Company. Must be graduate and must have an excellent command over spoken and written English. Should have at least 4 years experience in the relevant field. Apply to : The Managing Director ABC Electronics Limited, Okhla Industrial Area, Phase II, New Delhi.

13. You need two stenographers for your office. Write an advertisement for the 'Situations Vacant' column of a local newspaper.

SITUATIONS VACANT

A private Limited Company requires two stenographers for its office. The candidates should have at least three years experience and must have an excellent command over spoken and written English, besides having good shorthand and typing speed. Apply to Box 2076, the Hindustan Times, New Delhi-110001.

14. You are a graduate having experience in keeping Accounts. You need a job. Prepare an advertisement for publication in the 'Situations Wanted' column of a newspaper.

SITUATIONS WANTED

An energetic young graduate having five years experience of keeping Accounts is looking for full-time job. Box 38920 CA the Hindustan Times, New Delhi-110001.

15. You are a retired Major from the Indian Army having considerable Administration experience. Prepare an advertisement for publication in the local daily in the 'Situations Wanted' column.

SITUATIONS WANTED

A retired Army Major having 15 years experience in Administration is looking for a suitable placement. Please write to Box 381102, The Hindustan Times, New Delhi-110001.

16. You are working in a Limited Company as a Company Secretary. You are looking for a change. Prepare a suitable Advertisement for the 'SITUATIONS WANTED' column of the local daily.

SITUATIONS WANTED

A Company Secretary, having 9 years relevant experience, presently working in a Limited Company is looking for a suitable change. Please write to Box 110389 the Hindustan Times, New Delhi-110001.

EXERCISES FOR PRACTICE

1. Prepare a short classified advertisement for the 'Lost and Found' column of the newspaper stating the loss of your briefcase containing important documents.

2. You have lost your pet dog. Draft a suitable advertisement in about 25 words to be published in the 'LOST AND FOUND' column of a newspaper.
3. Write out a matrimonial advertisement for publication in a newspaper for a suitable match for your daughter.
4. You want to sell your car. Write a suitable advertisement in about 25 words to be printed in the 'FOR SALE' column of a newspaper.
5. You want to start a printing press. Draft an advertisement in about 25 words seeking a suitable building on rent to be published in 'WANTED ON RENT' column of a newspaper.
6. You are the Personnel Manager of a Five-star Hotel. You need a lady receptionist for the hotel. Write an advertisement for publication in a newspaper.
7. You need two typists for your office. Write an advertisement for the 'SITUATIONS VACANT' column of a local daily.
8. You need two lady checkers and one computer operator for your Export House. Draft an advertisement for a local daily.
9. You are on M.B.A. having 3 years managerial experience. Draft a suitable advertisement for the 'SITUATIONS WANTED' column of a local daily.
10. You lost your bus pass in the school. Give details of the pass and the probable time of the day you lost it. Your description should fit for the 'LOST AND FOUND' Notice Board of your school.
11. You are the Executive Manager of Metals and Minerals Corporation of India, New Delhi. Draft an advertisement to be published in a newspaper inviting offers from house-owners for suitable

accommodation on rent to be used as a guest house by the Corporation.

12. You need a receptionist and two computer operators for your office. Prepare a suitable advertisement for the local newspaper.
13. Prepare an advertisement for publication in the newspaper to let out your house. Give complete details of the building, nature of accommodation and rent expected.
14. You need an Office Assistant for your office. The candidate should have basic knowledge of computer and must be a graduate. Prepare a suitable advertisement for the local newspaper.
15. You need a suitable match for your son. Prepare a suitable advertisement for the Matrimonial column of a local newspaper.
16. While travelling by bus in your town you lost a bag containing your certificates. Write a classified advertisement for the 'LOST AND FOUND' column of a newspaper. Furnish all the details : the date and time of your journey, the bus service and the route, description of the bag etc.
17. You need a tutor for Maths for XII class. Prepare an advertisement for the local daily.
18. As the Principal of Laxman Public School, Haus Khas Enclave, New Delhi-110016, draft an advertisement to be given in the daily newspaper inviting applications for the post of librarian in your school.
19. You need a Junior Secretary for the Sales Department of your export house. Write an advertisement for the 'SITUATIONS VACANT' column of a local daily.
20. You are working as Assistant Manager with Standard Chartered Bank. Draft an advertisement for a newspaper seeking a change of job.